The Transformational Power of Purpose

Finding & Fulfilling Your Purpose in Life

The Transformational Power of Purpose
Finding & Fulfilling Your Purpose in Life

By Jim Whitt
Copyright ©2002

ISBN 0-9770004-1-9

Published by Lariat Press
www.lariatpress.com
1-800-874-4928

Table of Contents

Introduction

In the film *Unbreakable,* Bruce Willis plays the role of seemingly ordinary everyday man David Dunn. His ordinary life takes a turn for the extraordinary when he walks away from a train crash without a scratch and as the sole survivor. This is the first in a series of events that leads him to believe he possesses unique superhuman powers. He discovers that he is, in fact, a real life superhero. With this revelation he begins to conform to his true identity and fulfill his superhuman purpose.

It's a great storyline for a movie because it appeals to the human fascination with the supernatural. We want to believe there is something beyond the mundane and the ordinary. So, the human imagination creates superheroes who find their way into literature and film. And we buy the comic books and movie tickets because of some unexplainable desire to connect with these characters that are human and yet possess superhuman powers. Destiny has called them out for some magnificent purpose. They have important assignments to fulfill on planet earth.

What if you, like David Dunn, are a superhero but just simply haven't discovered your true identity? What if *you* possess supernatural abilities and destiny is waiting for you to accept your calling?

If you believe that *you* have a calling or a destiny in life, you're not alone. Life@Work Magazine surveyed more than 1,000 working American adults and asked if they believed they had a specific calling or destiny in life. While 84 percent believed there is a calling or destiny in their life, 64 percent felt they were not following that calling.

When asked more specifically whether or not a job can be included in that calling, 80 percent agreed that at some level it is. But only 34 percent really believed they were following their calling in their current job.

Life@Work concluded "that American adults do subscribe to the idea of having a calling or a destiny in life, but that it doesn't necessarily have an effect on the decisions they make."

We *want* to believe we have a calling, a destiny, a purpose. We intuitively feel that we are here on planet earth to do something specific, to carry out an assignment. We want to fulfill our destiny but struggle to hear our calling. The resulting frustration is probably best described by Henry David Thoreau who observed, "Most men lead lives of quiet desperation and go to the grave with their song still in them."

Thoreau's observation of the human condition in the 19th Century is still valid today. The mass of humanity is not wildly desperate, just *quietly* desperate — quietly but desperately seeking their calling, their destiny, the reason for their being in this world. It may not necessarily be a conscious quest but a voice deep inside of us keeps telling us we're here to fulfill a specific purpose.

That voice deep inside of us belongs to a *superhuman* trapped inside our mild-mannered mortal bodies crying out to be liberated, "Hey, it's me — the real you. I'm faster than a speeding bullet, more powerful than a locomotive and can leap tall buildings in a single bound. But I am *bound* by the kryptonite of purposelessness. Free me so I can fulfill my destiny!"

While your superhuman may not have X-ray vision or be able to bend steel with its bare hands it nevertheless possesses unique supernatural abilities. Your superhuman, the real you, is waiting to be liberated so you can complete your assignment.

I know the feeling. I was quietly desperate for 35 years, 6 months and 16 days of my life. I wanted to fulfill my destiny but was struggling to hear my calling. And the answer had to be more specific than an ambiguous generalization. I was not searching for *a* purpose in life or *the* purpose of life — I was searching for *my* purpose in life. And when I discovered that purpose — I was liberated. It was the beginning of an evolutionary metamorphosis that continues to this day. That discovery set me on a collision course with my destiny. My life became *electric*.

The Process

If a tree falls in the forest, and no one is there to hear, does it make a sound? The tree of purpose has fallen in the forest of destiny releasing the sound of your calling. Can you hear it? Not yet? That's OK. Your calling is like a radio signal carried on the airwaves of a specific frequency. Your purpose is calling you. You just have to get tuned in to the right frequency. I'll help you. I wrote this book to serve as the catalyst to free the superhuman in you. I'm going to share with you what I've learned about *the transformational power of purpose*. You're about to begin the process of getting tuned in.

This is an archaeological process of self-discovery. It will require you to dig deep inside of yourself. *You* have to find your purpose — no one else can tell you what it is. It's like the scene from *Forrest Gump* where Forrest, sitting at his mother's death-bed, asks, "What's my destiny, Mama?" His mother says simply, "You're gonna have to figure that out for yourself." Your purpose isn't something you *define*, it's something you *find*.

This process is kind of like playing the board game Clue. If you've played before, you'll remember that you search for clues to the murder by asking questions of the other players as you navigate the board. Finally the evidence leads you to conclude that Professor Plum committed the crime in the billiard room and the weapon was the candlestick. In this game however, each chapter will be a step in building a case for what your purpose is.

At the end of each chapter you'll complete an exercise. Here is a critical bit of advice. When completing the exercise, the objective is *not* to be brief and concise. The objective is to turn your mind loose so that it may find what you are seeking. Free yourself from any judgmental thinking as you write your responses. Write in as much detail as possible. In other words, don't discount anything that pops into your mind no matter how irrelevant it might seem. Your responses will contain the clues that will lead you to the discovery of your purpose.

God created you for a *specific* purpose. Ask him for supernatural insight as you read this book and complete the exercises. Ask him to make his voice very clear to you as he reveals your purpose to you. Your mind will subconsciously be seeking answers as you read this book and even when you aren't. You'll get flashes of inspiration when you least expect it. Be prepared, these insights occur spontaneously and when you might least expect them. When you do, write them down. They will provide the trail of evidence you need in solving the case for finding and fulfilling your purpose in life.

Enter into this process with a sense of expectancy. You are about to make a discovery that will transform your life. The superhuman in you is about to be liberated.

PS: This book is extremely effective when used in a small group process. To learn how to facilitate this process go to www.purposepower.org.

Chapter 1

The Road *Most* Traveled

"Two roads diverged in the wood," wrote Robert Frost. And I — I took the one less traveled by. And that has made all the difference." I was on the road *most* traveled — the road traveled by the quietly desperate masses Thoreau described. Then one day I stopped and asked, "Wait a minute, where am I going?" I was tired of the rat race. The rat race is a perpetual event on the road most traveled. I was tired of competing with all the other rats. So what if I was ahead of the rat behind me — there was another rat ahead of me. And where is the finish line in the rat race anyway?

I was frustrated. Feeling like a V-8 engine only hitting on four cylinders, I knew I had more talent and ability than I was using. I knew I could go faster and further than my little rat legs were carrying me but I didn't know *where* to run. It wasn't so much a case of knowing what I wanted to do, as it was a case of knowing what I *didn't* want to do. And I didn't want to do what I was doing anymore. So, I quit my job. Family and friends thought I was crazy and before I found what I was searching for, I began to think I was crazy, too.

I worked for Central Soya, an agribusiness firm headquartered in Fort Wayne, Indiana. Fort Wayne isn't a big city by most standards but it was a big city to me. And, as far as I was concerned, the rat race was synonymous with the city. My wife, Sondra, and I wanted to get back to our rural roots in Oklahoma where we had grown up in Mayberryesque settings. Sondra's hometown was a teeming metropolis of about 300 souls. I was from a big city relatively speaking, a town of about 700 people situated in the heart of Osage County, which had the unique distinction of being home to the largest population of cows in the state, and the oil field that put Phillips Petroleum on the map.

This was the first time I had been without a real job since college. After graduating from Oklahoma State University I went into sales with the Ralston Purina Company. I didn't just sell Dog Chow® and Cat Chow® — I sold cow chow. Most of my customers were large commercial cattle feeding operations located in the high plains of Kansas, Oklahoma and Texas. After ten years with Purina I spent a couple of years as the national cattle product marketing manager with Central Soya.

I decided to start my own business. My business plan was to do contract marketing for some former customers of mine when I worked for Purina and supplement my income by grazing and feeding cattle.

We wanted to live in the country where we could have some hogs, dogs and a few cows. Some friends of Sondra's folks had an empty farmhouse situated on a small acreage that sounded like it might fit the bill. I had never laid eyes on this place so I had to rely on Sondra's judgment since she had grown up a few miles down the road from there. She said it wasn't anything fancy but described it as livable. The most critical question in my mind was how much was the rent? She said they weren't going to charge us any rent. That answered all of my questions. As far as I was concerned, I didn't need to see this house, the price was right.

So we loaded up the kids and headed back to Oklahoma where, in the words of Rodgers and Hammerstein, the wind comes sweeping down the plain.

No more rat race.

I'll never forget the morning I first saw the farmhouse we were going to get to live in for free. It gave new meaning to "you get exactly what you pay for." Remember *Green Acres*? Well, Green Acres looked like a palace compared to this place. Eva Gabor would have divorced Eddie Albert before she would have moved into this house. To call it rundown would be too kind. It was dilapidated. The roof was sagging, the porch was sagging, and after seeing the house I was sagging, too. But being a positive thinking person, I told myself it had to be better on the inside.

I was wrong.

The ceiling was falling in because the roof leaked. It had no air conditioning and the main source of heat was a wood-burning stove. The living room was a long, narrow room covered with carpet — that ugly green and orange shag carpet that was so popular around 1970. It must have been designed by someone who was on a bad LSD trip. And as I stood on that green and orange shag carpet pondering our future, the two-by-four of reality hit me square between the eyes. *What in the world have I done? I've quit my job and I'm moving my family into a shack.*

I turned to Sondra and asked, "Are you *sure* you want to live here?" Remember, she was the one who picked this place out. Surely, it was a moment of temporary insanity and now, clothed and in her right mind she would say, "Of course not!" Instead she calmly replied, "Jim, we can live here temporarily."

I now had a headache and felt nauseous.

We drove back to my in-laws' house to spend the night. I woke up hoping this had just been a bad dream. It wasn't. We moved in. When we turned out the lights that first night we heard noises in the attic. Something was crawling around up there. No, something was scurrying. Rats — big rats.

The rat race had followed me and had taken up residence in our attic.

Murphy's Law

Our *temporary* stay at Green Acres turned out to be eighteen months — the longest ten years of my life. This house exceeded my expectations. It was *worse* than I had imagined.

In the winter it was so cold we could see our breath in the morning until we got a fire built. The water pipes froze under the house and burst. I chopped firewood until I thought my arms would fall off. Then I burned anything I could find, cut up and fit in the stove — old fence posts, railroad ties, crates, pallets, you name it. If it wasn't nailed down it was liable to end up in the fire. I swore I'd never have a wood-burning fireplace again in my life. It was so hot in the summer we slept on cots on the porch. Living there was like a never-ending campout. I was beginning to think it would be better to be back in the rat race rather than to have to listen to it take place in the attic every night.

I ended up getting a masters degree in Murphy's Law — anything that could go wrong did — and at the worst possible time. At the end of six months I'd lost $30,000 in the cattle business and my marketing venture was a total failure. It was a humbling experience. Feeling defeated and humiliated, I sank into a deep state of depression. I started asking the *why* and *how* questions. Why did I do this and how could I be so stupid? The why and how questions were followed by the *what* question. What am I going to do now?

It was during this time of not-so-quiet desperation that Sondra pulled into the drive one day and unloaded a cage with three chickens inside. She had wanted chickens ever since we moved to the country. Being a cattleman, I didn't have any great affinity for chickens and I told her we weren't buying any. She smiled and explained that she didn't *buy* them — the neighbors had given them to her. I thought this displayed a great deal of intelligence on their part.

And I was right. All three were roosters. Roosters don't lay eggs which, as far as I was concerned, were the best part of a chicken. I wondered how I could get rid of them without getting a divorce. An unlikely ally came to my aid.

The natural enemy of a chicken is a coyote. And we had plenty of coyotes. You could hear them howl every night when the sun went down. Within a week, two of the roosters had not so mysteriously disappeared. I patiently waited for the coyotes to usher the sole survivor of the three Roosterteers on to the big chicken coop in the sky. He must have narrowly escaped the jaws of death one night because he showed up one morning missing all his tail feathers. The coyotes couldn't kill this bird. This was one tough chicken. So now all that was left of our little family flock was one bobtailed Leghorn rooster.

The kids named him Elmer.

Elmer literally ruled the Green Acres roost. He bullied the dogs and cats into letting him sleep on the front porch with them. Roosting on the front porch created an environmental problem. While the dogs and cats preferred to do their business elsewhere Elmer decorated the porch in a style that made the shag carpet look appealing. That porch was an important part of the house since it was our bedroom on sultry summer nights.

If the coyotes couldn't take care of Elmer on their own I decided I would have to help them.

Wanting to be humane, I tried to trap Elmer. I propped up a box with a forked stick and baited the trap with a little corn. I tied a string around the stick and snuck off around the corner of the house and laid in wait for Elmer. I felt like Wile E. Coyote. And Elmer apparently thought he was the Roadrunner because he managed to peck a piece of corn and without as much as a "beep, beep" escaped before I could trip the stick. I felt a strong urge to call the Acme Corporation and order some roller skates and a rocket.

The elimination of Elmer became an obsession. I'd start my day plotting against him. I chased him off by peppering him with my son's BB gun but Elmer kept coming back. He was like the Energizer Bunny — he just kept going. *What did I have to do to get rid of this chicken?*

Early one morning, I was sipping my coffee watching the sunrise through the screen door on the back porch. I was contemplating the beauty of nature and thinking peaceful thoughts when the silhouette of a bobtailed rooster eclipsed the rising sun. I grabbed my Ruger 10/22 semi-automatic rifle, jammed in a ten shot clip, jacked in a shell and very quietly slipped out the door. Bracing myself against the woodshed, I drew a bead on Elmer.

It was too late. He spotted me and took off. I was right behind, running and stopping periodically to squeeze off a shot. Every time I fired, Elmer would jump and cluck. The chase took us around the garage and out into the front yard. I was running out of ammunition. Finally, with my last shot, I accomplished what the coyotes had only imagined in their dreams.

When I took off after Elmer, all I had on was my house shoes and my boxer shorts. So, here I was, standing over a dead chicken, dressed like an Aborigine and holding a smoking gun. I looked at the road in front of the house. Fortunately, no one was driving by.

The absurdity of what I had just done struck me. What if someone had witnessed my crime? *I saw the whole thing, officer. That's right. He was about six feet tall, 190 pounds. What was he wearing? Nothing but his BVDs and a smile — a sinister looking smile. He kind of reminded me of Wile E. Coyote. The chicken never had a chance.*

This was the low point of my life. I had a talk with myself. *You need to pull yourself together, Jim. You're losing it.*

I hand-delivered Elmer to the coyotes.

Back to the Future

The *why* and *how* questions wouldn't go away. And the question of *what to do now* would have to be answered soon if we were going to continue to buy groceries and pay bills. One cold winter's day during this time of soul searching, I was sorting through some old files. I pitched the ones I didn't want to keep into the wood-burning stove. Like I said, I burned anything I could find.

As I was sorting and burning, I opened up a folder that contained notes I had taken at a seminar. They were dated March 21, 1988. That would have been about a year earlier, nearly six months before I quit my job. At the top of one page I had written a thought-provoking question posed during that seminar — *what's your purpose in life?*

I can't tell you much about the seminar other than that one question. That's really all I can remember. But it was that question that took me on a journey in my mind's eye. We all have a mental VCR in our heads that records our past experiences and can replay them on demand. The *purpose* question punched the *play* button on mine and while sitting in the seminar I experienced a flashback from my days of selling feed with Purina.

If you've ever been in sales, you discover that prospects tend to have one word vocabularies and that one word is *no*. Your efforts are constantly met with doubt and defeat. Selling feed is no different. Some of those old cowboys who managed the feedlots didn't want to waste their time talking to salesmen so they did their dead level best to run them off. I was able to survive and even thrive largely in part because I had worked in feedyards. I had cowboyed for a living, understood the business, and spoke the managers' language.

Whenever I called on a manager for the first time I asked him a series of questions about his operation, thanked him for his time and headed on down the road. These questions were second nature to me and they started me off on the right foot with the manager. It was how I started building a relationship with a prospect. The questions were my way of finding out the biggest problems the manager was dealing with. My strategy was to then help the manager find solutions to those problems, even when they didn't have anything to do with the product I was selling. It was this simple approach that enabled me to become a top 20 producer in a sales force of 500.

My flashback featured a young salesman I had worked with named Mike. Mike was a sharp young guy but new to the business of selling to these large feedlots. He and I spent a couple of days working together, so I could share some of the tricks of the trade with him. As we were driving down the road between sales calls he looked over at me and said, "Jim, I don't like to admit this but I don't even know what questions to ask a feedlot manager on the first call." I told him to take out his pad and pen and start writing. While we zipped down the road that day somewhere out in the middle of nowhere, I rattled off the questions I always asked.

I never gave those questions or my day with Mike much thought again until a couple of years later when I left Purina to take the marketing job in Indiana. When Mike found out I was leaving the company he said he wanted to thank me for something. I'll never forget what he said, "I still have the ten questions Jim Whitt gave me to ask a feedlot manager on the first call." He thanked me for sharing those ten questions with him.

At that precise moment in my flashback, my mental VCR stopped the video and freeze-framed a close-up of Mike's face. The eyes are the windows to the soul, and as I looked into Mike's eyes, here's what I saw. Potential. I saw the tremendous potential Mike possessed. It occurred to me that all he needed was someone to show him the ropes, point him in the right direction and say, "You can do it." He just needed someone to help him reach the potential he already possessed. That's what I was doing — I was helping him reach *his* full potential.

As I sat by that wood-burning stove on that cold winter's day in that run-down old farmhouse, I looked at the answer I had written to the *purpose* question from a year earlier — *my purpose is to help people reach their full potential.*

That answered the *why* question. It was as if God said, "Good. You've figured it out. Now get ready because you're on a collision course with destiny." I was liberated. My life shifted into overdrive. I felt like the Blues Brothers — *I was on a mission for God*.

March 21, 1988, is a red-letter date on my calendar because that's when I discovered the reason for my being. I didn't know the impact that day would have on my life until I found that file with my notes almost a year after the fact. I wrote my purpose on a piece of paper, stuck it into a file folder and never gave it much thought. But that set supernatural forces in motion.

Looking back on it, I didn't really understand why I was quitting my job, starting my own business and moving into that old farmhouse. I just thought I wanted out of the rat race and to get back to my rural roots. But the power of purpose was pulling me like a magnet and I didn't even know it.

Although I discovered my purpose long before we moved to Green Acres, it was there I began experiencing *the transformational power of purpose*. The talents and abilities I felt were underutilized were now beginning to be maximized and I discovered some I never knew I possessed. I started the process of *being* exactly what I was designed and assigned to do. People and circumstances began to come together at exactly the right time, enabling and empowering me to fulfill my purpose. It was the beginning of a journey that has taken me places I hadn't planned to go, to do things I hadn't planned to do and experience things I could have never imagined.

I felt a little like David Dunn in *Unbreakable*. I was an ordinary human being who was coming to the realization that something about me wasn't so ordinary. I didn't fully understand it yet but the *real me* was beginning to surface.

The superhuman in me was being set free.

For 35 years, 6 months and 16 days of my life I was on the road *most* traveled. Then one day I stopped and asked for directions. I discovered my purpose and that started my journey on the road *less* traveled.

And Robert Frost is right — it does make all the difference.

Your Autobiography

As I look back over my life I'm now able to see how everything I've experienced has prepared me to fulfill my purpose. I can see a trail of clues that, when viewed in retrospect, provide critical insights to my purpose. I was destined to help people reach their full potential and my life's experiences provided the perfect training ground.

Your life, when viewed in retrospect, leaves a trail of clues that provide critical insights to your purpose. Your life's experiences have provided the perfect training ground for you to fulfill your purpose.

Write your autobiography from birth to today — in condensed form, of course. Include all of the significant experiences — regardless of whether you consider them to be positive or negative — that have helped make you who you are today. Conclude your biography by completing this sentence — *the most significant thing about me is...*

_____

_____

_____

_____

_____

_____

_____

_____

_____

_____

_____

_____

_____

_____

_____

Your Autobiography: Continued

_____
_____
_____
_____
_____
_____
_____
_____
_____
_____
_____
_____
_____
_____
_____
_____
_____
_____
_____
_____
_____
_____
_____
_____
_____

Your Autobiography: Continued

_____

_____

_____

_____

_____

_____

_____

_____

_____

_____

_____

_____

_____

_____

_____

_____

_____

_____

_____

_____

_____

_____

_____

_____

Chapter 2

Why Are *You* Crossing the Road?

In the film City Slickers, Mitch (Billy Crystal) is a New York radio ad salesman experiencing a midlife crisis. He and his two closest friends, who are pretty much in the same boat, decide that a cattle drive on a dude ranch is the perfect vacation. My favorite scene is when Curly (Jack Palance), the tougher-than-nails old cowboy, is riding along with Mitch looking for strays:

Curly: How old are you? Thirty-eight?

Mitch: Thirty-nine.

Curly: You all come up here about the same age, same problems. You spend about fifty weeks a year gettin' knots in your rope and then you think two weeks up here will untie 'em for you. None of you get it.

You know what the secret of life is?

Mitch: No, what?

Curly: This (holding up his index finger).

Mitch: Your finger?

Curly: One thing. Just one thing. You stick to that and everything else don't mean s____.

Mitch: That's great but what's the one thing?

Curly: That's what you gotta figure out.

I can relate to Mitch. I had my rope all tied up in knots but after a year-and-half at Green Acres I had figured it out. The *one thing* was finding my purpose. I was put here on earth *to help people reach their full potential*. Now that I knew my destination in life I was ready to roll on the road less traveled. All I needed now was a vehicle to get me there.

One of my clients from my failed marketing venture provided me with one. Mel headed up the largest family-owned agricultural enterprise in the state of Kansas and was a stockholder in many other businesses. One day he and I were visiting about the challenges of managing his ever growing enterprise and he said they needed help. He pointed out the fact that I had several years of experience working for two major corporations and that maybe I could advise them.

19

That's how I became a management consultant.

Mel was one of the people put in my path to help me fulfill my purpose. He was able to see something in me that I wasn't even able to see in myself. My purpose of helping people reach their full potential *pulled* me into the personal and organizational development business that I'm still engaged in today.

I had evolved all the way from cow puncher to people provoker. My degree in animal science and a lifetime of working in the livestock industry had prepared me to understand human behavior from a very unique perspective. That's not exactly the education and career path most people take to become a management consultant. It's not the path I would have chosen but that's the transformational power of purpose.

Discovering my purpose has helped me put my past into perspective. The good, the bad and yes, even the ugly chapters of my life have provided the necessary experience I needed to fulfill my purpose. The path of purpose may not always make sense in the present tense but it makes perfect sense when viewed in the past tense. In the words of Danish philosopher Soren Kierkegaard, "Life must be lived forward but understood backward."

Cowboy Psychology

My wife eventually joined me as a partner in our business. She has a masters degree in industrial/organizational psychology. I've always jokingly said that when it comes to dealing with people, my degree in animal science works better. But the mapping of the human genome may have given some validity to my assertion. Only three percent of the genetic pool makes up the human genes. Humans share 75% of the same genes with a rat and 98.4% of the same genes with a chimpanzee. That's encouraging, isn't it? If it weren't for a 1.6% difference in your DNA you'd be sharing a banana with a chimp right now.

Now that we've established the fact that we share much of the same gene pool with rats and monkeys, let's drill a little deeper. What *separates* us from other animals? To answer that question I've developed what I call *Cowboy Psychology.*

To understand Cowboy Psychology let's explore the age-old conundrum that has perplexed the human species for centuries, "Why did the chicken cross the road?" The stock answer is, "To get to the other side." But *why* did the chicken want to get to the other side? What was the chicken's *motivation*? As you can tell, my experience with Elmer led me to delve deep into the poultry psyche.

Motivate means "to *stimulate* to action." The root word of motivate is *motive.* Therefore, motivation requires a motive. For the chicken, there are only two possible motives to cross the road. One, there is something on its side of the road it is trying to get away from (pain or punishment) or two, there is something on the other side of the road it is trying to get to (pleasure or reward). In other words, the chicken is merely responding to pain or pleasure. The stimuli of reward and punishment can be used to *motivate* the chicken. Provide the appropriate stimulus and the chicken responds.

I can train *any* animal using these two stimuli.

After much repetition the animal's behavior becomes a conditioned response to the stimulus or some other trigger that's associated with the stimulus. This is what psychologists call *classical* or *operant conditioning.*

To train an animal to repeat a specific behavior, some type of reward is used as a stimulus. If you've ever been to Sea World you've seen Shamu, the killer whale, perform tricks such as jumping through a hoop. For properly performing a trick, Shamu is rewarded with a couple of fish.

Shamu has been fed a small ocean full of fish to keep him jumping through the hoop. And to keep Shamu performing these tricks the reward must always be waiting at the end. If the trainer stops feeding Shamu the fish for jumping through the hoop, Shamu stops jumping through the hoop. To get Shamu to perform an even more difficult trick, the trainer will increase the degree of stimulation. In Shamu's case that means more fish.

To train an animal to discontinue a specific behavior, punishment is used as a stimulus. A dog trainer will often use a shock collar for this purpose. The collar is equipped with an electrical shock mechanism that is activated by remote control. All the trainer has to do is push a button on the remote and an electrical shock is delivered via two electrodes on the collar. After several repetitions the dog associates the behavior with the shock and becomes conditioned to discontinue the behavior. And Shamu is glad no one has found a shock collar big enough to fit him.

I use a shock collar as a prop in my presentations to help explain the use of aversive stimuli (pain or punishment) in the conditioning process. After one of my conditioning lessons someone in the audience came up to me and told me a story about his friend — we'll call him Bubba — who encountered a problem while using a shock collar to train his bird dog. It seems Bubba's dog was not responding to the shock. He reasoned that either the shock collar was defective or the dog had developed a resistance to the shock, which will sometimes happen. This is not unusual. While aversive stimuli may be a powerful short-term stimulus, animals may become desensitized to the pain.

Bubba decided to enlist his wife of 30 years to help him test his collar. Yep, you guessed it, Bubba asked her to put on the collar and he would push the button on the remote to see if it was working. She agreed but asked if they might reverse roles. Why didn't he put on the collar and she would operate the remote? Bubba, not being the sharpest knife in the drawer, agreed as long as she followed his instructions to the letter.

Bubba explained that he was going down into the pasture a couple of hundred yards and would be out of earshot, so he would signal when he wanted her to push the button. The signal would be waving his hands above his head in an abbreviated jumping-jack motion. "*Anytime* I wave my hands," Bubba insisted, "you push the button. Understand?"

He strapped the collar on, cinched it up tight and walked the distance of two football fields into the pasture. He then turned and waved his hands enthusiastically. His wife pushed the button.

The shock collar worked all too well. Upon being electrocuted (a non-lethal shock, of course, but nonetheless very stimulating) his muscles contracted violently. This caused him to throw his arms up into the air and wave his hands again but with even more enthusiasm. This was probably one part physiological response and one part a very desperate attempt on Bubba's behalf to try and remove the collar.

Apparently Bubba's long suffering bride had 30 years of frustration pent up inside and saw what might best be described as a window of opportunity. Mindful to follow Bubba's instructions to the letter, she pushed the button every time he waved his hands.

It seems she kept Bubba dancing, and herself entertained, for quite some time.

Now, for *the rest of the story* as Paul Harvey would say. I never use a *real* shock collar in my presentations. I use what's called a *dummy* collar. Once a dog is effectively conditioned to respond to a shock collar, it can be replaced with a dummy. The dummy looks just like a shock collar with one small but very important difference — the dummy collar can't shock the dog. But the dog doesn't know that — so it behaves exactly as it has been conditioned.

I use this story to make a point. We humans are all wearing invisible dummy collars. Even though we may not be subjected to the *shock* of a real collar we are conditioned from infancy to respond to reward and punishment. The first word we *heard* and *understood* coming out of our parent's mouths was, "NO!" This was accompanied with a slap on the hand — or somewhere else on our anatomies. This was the first step in our behavioral conditioning using aversive stimuli (punishment, pain).

Your early developmental conditioning included stimuli that resulted in pleasure as well as pain. If you were a good little boy or girl you were rewarded with a piece of candy, a cookie or a toy. Shades of Shamu.

The conditioning process continues through our childhood in our formal education and into adulthood as we enter the workforce. By the time we reach legal age we are well trained animals.

Pavlov's Humans

Behaviorism is a theory asserting that psychology is essentially a study of *external* human behavior rather than *internal* consciousness and desires. While most of us are familiar with Russian psychologist Ivan Pavlov's experiments in conditioning (Pavlov's dogs) it was the American psychologist, B.F. Skinner, who stressed the similarities between human and animal learning processes. Skinner and other *behaviorists* associated an arbitrary action (such as an animal pressing a lever) with a reward (presentation of food) or a punishment (an electric shock).

We humans are trained just like any other animal using reward, punishment or combinations of the two.

We not only are trained like animals we also learn to play the roles of Siegfried & Roy. We graduate from trainee to trainer. Parents become master animal trainers. Teenagers are the ultimate test of their skills. And the most difficult of all tricks to teach the teenager is getting them to clean their own rooms. They've tried reward as a stimulus — only to discover they'll go broke. They've tried punishment — but they can only ground them until they're 21.

In either case, the *motivation* was short lived. Why? Reward and punishment are more *manipulation* than motivation. You have to continually provide the stimulus to get the response. And you always have to increase the degree of stimulation — more reward or more punishment — because humans, just like Bubba's bird dog, become desensitized to the stimuli.

The real reason teenagers aren't *motivated* to clean their rooms is because they see absolutely no *purpose* in it. *Why should I clean my room? It'll only get dirty again.*

Here's the other side of this coin. One Saturday in April, when our son was a junior in high school, he washed, waxed and cleaned our car until it looked showroom perfect and you know why. It was prom night and he wanted to borrow the car. We didn't have to reward him or punish him to do this because he had a *purpose*.

This leads us to the single most important principle I've discovered about human motivation: *Without a purpose, our only motivation is reward and punishment.* This is the fundamental tenet of Cowboy Psychology.

Why Are *You* Crossing the Road?

Let's get back to the question of what separates us from other animals. We know why the chicken crossed the road. Now, let's make it personal — why are *you* crossing the road? What's your *motive*? Is it reward? Is it punishment? If so, you can be manipulated as easily as any other animal. As your trainer all I have to do is to find the stimulus that corresponds to the response I desire to elicit. And whenever I push that button I can make you dance just like Bubba. I just need to find out what's in your *schema*.

Schema is the root word of schematic. A schematic diagram is basically a map that reveals how something is constructed or wired. Schema is a term psychologists use to describe how *you* are wired. Your life's experiences are stored in schemas that are like maps of the *neurological pathways* in your mind.

Once a schema is fully formed it becomes *your* dummy collar. It's your filter for all incoming information. You do one of three things with incoming information filtered through your schemas. If it fits your schema you accept it. If it doesn't fit you reject it or reshape it to make it fit.

Permit me to play the role of animal trainer and I'll make you the subject of a little experiment. I'm going to strap a specially designed shock collar around your neck. This collar will send signals to *your* schema. Imagine your schema as a motion picture archive where you can retrieve videos to play in your mental VCR. I've got the remote. I can push certain buttons that play certain videos in your mind's eye that correlate to your past conditioning.

To manipulate you with reward and punishment all I have to do is find the right stimuli that appeal to your needs and fears.

What Are You Afraid Of?

We may be fearful of many different things but we all have five basic fears.

1. Fear of the unknown.
2. Fear of change.
3. Fear of failure.
4. Fear of success.
5. Fear of rejection.

What are you afraid of? Failure? Let me see — I think I'll play a video clip from when you were in little league. You are up to bat in the bottom of the last inning, with the bases loaded. There are two out and your team is down by three runs. The eyes of everyone in attendance — no, the eyes of the entire world — are all focused on you. The count is three balls and two strikes. Here's the pitch. It's right down the middle of the plate. You swing — and miss. Game lost. As you walk back to the dugout you see the disappointment in your teammates' eyes and hear the cheers of the opposing team.

How about fear of rejection? I'll push a button that retrieves a couple of other video clips from your childhood. The first clip features your older sister, the darling of the world. It's shot in Technicolor. She's Miss Personality, the head cheerleader, the homecoming queen, the straight A student, and yada, yada, yada…

Now I'll play a clip of you. It's a low budget black and white film. You play the real life role of a shy little girl, a reclusive soul, who spends hours hiding out in her room, lost in the pages of one of the many books that keep her company. She finds solace and acceptance in this shadow land where the only other inhabitants are the fictional characters in the pages of her books. Here she can be Miss Personality, the head cheerleader, the homecoming queen and the straight A student. But just outside the door of her room, the inhabitants of the real world ignore her. She is a mere distraction at best.

These experiences are indelibly etched into your schema. I can push your buttons and you will flinch mentally and emotionally. And if you ever wander beyond the boundaries of your fears, I can use them as effectively as a lion tamer armed with a chair and whip, and back you into your cage.

All of us have flashbacks when triggered by the right stimulus that are all too real and painful. These are effective tools in my arsenal of manipulation. There is a video clip for every one of your fears in your film archives. Some are horror films that feature full-blown phobias that are capable of paralyzing you. To manipulate you with fear in our experiment, all I have to do is find a clip of one of your fears and play it. Then I can use that as the stimulus for the response I desire from you.

OK, Enough of this punishment. There are endless examples of fears I could list. I could go on but I don't want to be sadistic.

What's Your Pleasure?

I have other ways to persuade you in our little experiment. Reward is a more pleasant stimulation, but just as manipulative in its effect. I'll use it to appeal to the *needs* imprinted in your schemas.

Psychologist Abraham Maslow developed a hierarchy of human needs that is taught in every basic psychology course. He divided needs into three major categories: Fundamental, Psychological and Self-Actualization.

The fundamental tier includes our most basic needs — food, shelter, sex and the need to feel safe, secure and out of danger.

The psychological category includes belonging: the need to affiliate with others and feel loved and accepted, and our esteem needs: achievement, competence and recognition.

The top rung of the hierarchal ladder is what Maslow called self-actualization — the need to fulfill our own unique potential.

It's not hard to find stimuli that appeal to your needs. Television commercials are filled with them so I'll use some for the next part of our experiment.

Some of the most creative ads on television are beer commercials. They have featured ants, frogs, lizards and a guy that says, "I love you man." But they rely on one tried and true stimulus they know will always appeal to the male psyche — women. And not just any women — they all look like Cindy Crawford clones. And how are they dressed? Barely.

These commercials always include a little eye candy for the ladies, too. These bikini clad Cindy Crawford clones are playing volleyball on the beach with men who all look like Arnold Schwarzenegger. Hey girls, this Bud's for you.

The stimuli in beer commercials are aimed at your fundamental needs. They don't sell beer by appealing to your thirst, they appeal to a more powerful appetite — sex. Does it work? Anheuser Busch thinks so.

Maslow's Hierarchy of Needs

SELF-ACTUALIZATION
Fulfilling One's Unique Potential

Achievement, Competence &
Recognition
PSYCHOLOGICAL
Affiliation with Others

To Feel Safe, Secure & Out of Danger
FUNDAMENTAL
Food, Shelter & Sex

How about your need for security? Complete this sentence. You're in good hands with _____. If you didn't say Allstate you've been living on another planet. That slogan has been indelibly imprinted in your schema from years of advertising.

Any good life insurance salesman will come to your home, sit across from you at your kitchen table and paint a picture in your mind's eye. It's a picture of you — lying in your coffin. You are now having an out of body experience viewing yourself at your own funeral. And while you are admiring yourself resting peacefully in your Sunday best the salesman shocks you back to planet earth with this perfectly timed and delivered question, "In the untimely event of your death (I've always wondered when the *timely* event would be) would your family be cared for?" This is the stimulus. The response is your signature on the dotted line.

Maslow said that once our fundamental needs are met we move up the hierarchy to our psychological needs. So what commercials appeal to our belonging needs? Would you believe McDonalds? McDonalds doesn't sell hamburgers in their commercials, they sell the experience of going to McDonalds. They market to different age and ethnic groups in different parts of the country. Their commercials feature little kids playing with Ronald McDonald. In Florida they put senior citizens in their commercials. In the southwest you'll see Hispanics in their commercials and in areas with predominately African-American populations, they feature black people. Their message is clear. It doesn't matter if you are young, old, black, white or from another planet — you *belong* at McDonalds. If you don't believe that, just try driving past the golden arches with the kids in the back seat. If you don't stop they'll let you know about it in eardrum bursting decibel levels.

Now, for our esteem needs. Nike commercials featured Michael Jordan performing super-human feats. How did he do it? It's the shoes man, it's the shoes. A pair of Air Jordans cost about $135. When I was a kid I wore U.S. Keds. I doubt my parents paid more than five bucks for my Keds. Do you really think kids can jump any higher in Air Jordans than they could in a pair of U.S. Keds? So why would anyone pay $130 more for Air Jordans? Because their commercials appeal to the need for achievement, competence and recognition. If we wear Nikes we'll run faster, jump higher and be the envy of our friends — we can be just like Mike.

Well, I think you've had enough. My experiment is over. During our experiment, your mental VCR played clips stored in your schematic archives didn't it? Fears and needs are imprinted in your schema and are associated with your life's experiences. Our five senses become engaged when a stimulus connects with past experiences. It is virtual reality. We relive these experiences in our mind's eye. We respond physiologically to the imagined experience much like we would to the real experience.

To stimulate you to action using reward all I have to do is find out what your dominant need is on the hierarchy. If it is food, shelter, sex and/or security, I can appeal to your physiological (animal) needs. If you are all about relationships, I appeal to belonging. If you are a high achiever I can appeal to your esteem needs.

As you move up the hierarchy you become more human. But I can't push any of your buttons to manipulate you into self-actualizing. Fulfilling your unique potential requires your *superhuman* to be engaged. What stimulus appeals to him?

Wouldn't you like to know how to be freed from the manipulation of reward and punishment? Are you tired of responding like other animals to the stimuli that constantly appeal to your needs and fears? Are you ready to liberate the superhuman that is held captive inside your animal body?

Then you'll want to learn how to walk *upright* in a four-legged world. I'll show you how in the next chapter.

Needs & Fears

Needs and fears play a legitimate role in our lives. They keep our animal bodies alive, well and functioning. But being controlled by our fears and deficiency needs (those at the bottom of Maslow's hierarchy) inhibits the evolution from mere mortal animal into superhuman. As we climb the ladder of Maslow's hierarchy we rise above our animal natures to fulfill our unique individual potential. Consider this as you complete this process. Record your responses to the following questions:

Where do you think you are, or spend most of your time, on Maslow's hierarchy?

_____

_____

_____

_____

_____

Do you feel like you are stuck at that level?

_____

_____

_____

_____

_____

Why do you think you are stuck?

_____

_____

_____

_____

_____

What is your greatest fear?

_____

_____

_____

_____

What is it that you want to do or need to take action on but are putting off because you don't think you have the time, money or ability to accomplish?

_____

_____

_____

_____

What fear or need is holding you back?

_____

_____

_____

_____

What's the first step you have to take to get started?

_____

_____

_____

_____

When will you take it?

_____

_____

_____

_____

_____

Chapter 3

Learning to Walk Upright in a Four-Legged World

A headline in an issue of *USA Today* caught my attention: "Firms spend billions to fire up workers — with little luck. There's no proof hot coals or speeches motivate the troops." The accompanying article chronicled some of the more creative ways companies try to motivate employees including shelling out big bucks to have employees walk barefoot across 1,500-degree coals.

I suppose they hope if you can walk across a bed of hot coals barefoot maybe you can hot foot it to work on time.

Some companies cited in the article relied on the more conventional attempts to pump up employees like bringing in a motivational speaker. But sadly, motivational speakers have become fodder for parodies. The late Chris Farley was hilarious on *Saturday Night Live* as Mac Foley, the overweight, underwhelming motivational speaker who lived in a van down by the river.

Motivational books, tapes, CDs and videos are a billion dollar industry. And then there are the posters, T-shirts, coffee mugs and anything else you can print a motivational message on.

But the message doesn't seem to be getting through. Consider the findings of a Gallup study cited in the article: "55% of employees have no enthusiasm for their work — Gallup uses the term *not engaged* — based on several criteria, including loyalty and the desire to improve job performance. It found that one in five (19%) are so uninterested or negative about their jobs that they poison the workplace to the point that companies might be better off if they called in sick."

Billions are spent to motivate employees yet nearly three-fourths of the workforce is unmotivated.

It's a Jungle Out There

How many times have you heard someone refer to their workplace as a zoo? It's not an entirely inaccurate description. Many corporate cultures are, in a very real sense, animal cultures. Reward and punishment continue to be the stimuli of choice to motivate people. But remember, that's not motivation, that's manipulation.

If people are manipulated like animals they tend to *naturally* respond like animals. A culture of reward and punishment is an animal's *natural* habitat. The result is organizations are

31

full of unmotivated people. And the corporate culture is merely a reflection of the culture at large, a culture filled with quietly desperate, unmotivated people.

The natural world is the four-legged world we live in. It's a jungle out there and your animal thrives in this natural habitat. Our animal bodies are subject to all of the needs and fears of any other animal. We are being constantly bombarded with pain (punishment) and pleasure (reward) stimuli. To be manipulated by reward and punishment is *natural*.

Your superhuman is frustrated because it is created to be more than an animal. It wants to be liberated, walk upright and conform to its divine nature — to be like its Creator.

So how can you learn to walk upright in this four-legged world?

Best-selling author Spencer Johnson believes research may one day show that the only long-lasting motivation will come from employees who bring it to work with them in the form of God, spirituality, or something else that causes them "to rise to a higher purpose." In other words, without a purpose our only motivation is reward and punishment.

To be truly motivated, we must tap into what separates us from animals. And here's where we'll part company with the behaviorists. We are created in the image of *God*. We are God-like creatures — *supernatural* beings — housed in the bodies of animals.

We are the only animals that have the ability to *choose* our behavior. All other animals are merely responding to *extrinsic* stimuli. Humans are the only animals with the capacity to be internally or *intrinsically* motivated. We choose to act or *not* act on a motive. When we respond to a stimulus we are being *reactive*. To choose to act on a motive is to be *proactive*.

Animals can't be motivated because they can't choose to act on a motive. They can only be *manipulated* by responding to a stimulus.

If you no longer want to be manipulated like an animal, your superhuman has to rule. To do that you have to understand that your superhuman doesn't respond to external stimuli. What it does respond to is *purpose*. Your superhuman thrives in a *supernatural* habitat. Your purpose *connects* you to this supernatural habitat. To be motivated by your purpose is *supernatural*. When you know and act on God's purpose for your life, you are the extension of God you were created to be.

It's like the *Force* in *Star Wars*. After Obi Wan Kenobi is killed by Darth Vader, it's up to Luke to save the day. Luke is caught between two worlds, the natural world he's always known and the supernatural world he's just starting to experience. It is at this critical juncture where he is trying to figure out what to do that he hears the voice of Obi Wan's spirit, "Relax, Luke and let the Force take over."

When we are *on purpose*, the Force flows through us, *supernaturally* empowering us to fulfill what we are called to do.

The superhuman in you is repulsed by manipulation, yet your animal body is conditioned to respond to reward and punishment. When we are merely responding to external stimuli it's like riding in a wagon pulled by a two-horse team. One horse is named Reward and the other is named Punishment. They battle each other trying to run in opposite directions, swerving from one side of the road to the other. It's a runaway team and you fight them, trying to rein them in. That's what life is like when you're *not* on purpose. It's a constant battle of the wills between these two horses.

When you're on purpose, you're *riding* one horse instead of *driving* two. That horse is named Purpose and he *knows* where to go. All you have to do is saddle up, give him his head and get in rhythm with him as you gallop purposefully towards your destination.

You can relax, and let the Force take over.

Being Directionally Correct

We admire high achievers, those who set high goals and attain them. Achievement, competence and recognition are not necessarily bad but we can't assume that reaching the esteem level of Maslow's hierarchy brings with it happiness and fulfillment. Many high achievers are obsessed with getting to the top only to find it wasn't all it was cracked up to be. Even Madonna, the self-proclaimed "Material Girl" found life at the top to be a letdown. The study of Kabbalah, an offshoot of Judaism, led her to reevaluate her material ways, "I was super-ambitious, super-hardworking and super-focused, and I've gotten a lot of good things I wanted. But I now know the whole point of being here isn't to be at the top of the list."

Setting goals when you don't know your purpose is like trying to map out a route when you don't know where you're going. We *naturally* set and achieve goals everyday. It's the way we're designed. You set goals to get up in the morning, go to work, go home and go to bed. Did you achieve your goals today? Sure you did. What happens when you set a goal and achieve it? You set and achieve another one.

But where are your goals taking you? You may be like the test pilot who radioed in and announced he had no idea where he was going but was making really good time. When you don't know what your purpose is, you don't know if you are directionally correct.

Being at the top of the list doesn't translate to fulfilling your purpose. You can be successful and still be unfulfilled. Your *success* may merely be the result of being *driven* (remember the two-horse team) by your fears and/or needs.

As you evolve from *manipulated animal* to *motivated superhuman*, you move to the top of Maslow's hierarchy and begin to self-actualize. You are now on the path of fulfilling your own *unique* potential. And you may discover talents and abilities you never even knew you possessed.

When I was punching cows or selling feed, I could not have possibly dreamed that someday I would be writing books or giving advice to people as a management consultant. Believe me, getting paid for giving speeches wasn't anywhere on my radar screen when I got a paddling for talking *too* much in the first grade. I was on the road to fulfilling my purpose at an early age and my teacher tried to beat it out of me.

Are You Self-Actualizing?

Maslow believed the self-actualizing individual exhibited the following characteristics:

1. Being independent of others' opinions.
2. Being detached from the outcome.
3. Having no investment in power or control over others.

I've found these self-actualizing qualities to be *byproducts* of being on purpose. When we are on purpose we are intrinsically motivated, so we become increasingly less susceptible to extrinsic stimuli that appeal to our needs and fears.

All of the needs on the hierarchy are legitimate. My animal has to be fed. But when I am motivated by my purpose, my animal is kept on a short leash and my superhuman *holds* that leash. My superhuman leads my animal instead of my animal leading my superhuman.

Purpose puts our fears and needs in their proper order. While they are necessary for our survival they should not control us.

Being on purpose empowers me to:

1. Be independent of others' opinions because I know what my purpose is and fulfilling my purpose is more important than what other people think of me. Someone will always try to put you into a box of who you are supposed to be and what you are supposed to do. When you know you're on purpose the fear of rejection diminishes.

2. Be detached from the outcome because the outcome is in God's hands and not mine. I'm in the efforts business and God is in the results business. I don't get upset if the results don't match my expectations. I can let the path of purpose take me where I'm supposed to go instead of where I think I want to go.

3. Have no investment in power or control over others because what I want is not important. Fulfilling my purpose is important. If the outcome is in God's hands, why should I feel the need to manipulate others? As I act on my purpose, I've discovered that people come to me at appointed times when I need help.

When I am on purpose I can relax and let the Force take over.

Self-Actualization is not self-absorption. It is its opposite. It enables you to live inside out instead of outside in. Your focus shifts from being self-serving to simply serving. You see yourself as being a part of something bigger than you are. The world no longer revolves around what *you* want. You instead see yourself as having something unique to offer and you want to be a giver rather than a taker.

"True happiness is not attained through self-gratification," said Helen Keller, "but through fidelity to a worthy purpose."

A Superhuman Race

The transformational power of purpose is the catalyst that starts an evolutionary process:

- From conception through our early childhood we are totally dependent. We depend on our parents and others.
- As we mature we learn *independence*. We learn to do for ourselves.
- We struggle with the next step of the maturation process — *interdependence*. Our animal bodies are completely self-obsessed. I want what I want. But as humans we are created to be *interdependent*.

Nothing demonstrates this more than how people respond in the wake of a disaster. On September 11, 2001 our world was rocked with surreal images of the World Trade Towers collapsing in flames. We gathered around television sets and watched in disbelief. That was followed by the attack on the Pentagon, the very heart of our armed forces.

Our world changed that day — it got a lot heavier. I thought about that old Eddie Arnold song: "Make the world go away and get it off my shoulders…"

In Greek mythology it was Atlas who was charged with shouldering the weight of the world. Although Atlas was one of the legendary Titans, a race of gods, he decided the burden was too much to bear. Exhibiting not-so-god-like character, he tried to trick Hercules into assuming his task, but failed. Atlas couldn't make the world go away and neither can we.

In the aftermath of the terrorist attacks we not only prayed to God, we questioned God. How could God allow this to happen? How could these terrorists kill and destroy in the name of God?

The terrorists responsible for the deaths of thousands of people proved that there are those who *choose* to be no more than animals. But we must also remember our animal bodies serve host to a race of superhumans created in the image of God.

If there is anything positive to come from times of great tragedy it is that they provoke us to rise above our animal natures and assume the likeness of our Creator. In the words of Cicero, "Men resemble God never so much as in doing good to their fellow creatures." It is in these times of tragedy that the part of us that is God reaches out to the other members of our superhuman race.

In the days following the attacks, the images of explosions and implosions gave way to images of firefighters, police and volunteers working side by side, day and night; images of people donating food, clothing, money and their own blood; images of those who gathered all across America and the world to pray. It is in these images that we saw the true image of God.

These times of crisis give us a glimpse, if but for a brief shining moment, of what happens when the human spirit is liberated to assume superhuman status. This should not be the exception, it should be the rule. It is the way we are created to live. Not just in times of crisis, but daily. Unfortunately, when the crisis subsides, we see the mass of humanity revert back to their animal natures and once again fall prey to the manipulation of reward and punishment.

Atlas was at a disadvantage. He alone was charged with carrying the weight of the world. He had no one to share the task. We possess power far superior to the Titans of Greek mythology. In times of great crisis we become one heart and mind as we stand shoulder to shoulder with the brothers and sisters of our superhuman race to do good to our fellow creatures. And together, upon these many shoulders, we are able to lift the weight of the world.

The Force is with us.

Individually we make a difference, but together we can perform miracles. We are part of a great play and each of us plays an important role. In the words of William Shakespeare, "The world is a stage and all the people players."

What role are you supposed to play?

Your Very Best

There are times in our life when we feel as though we are really alive. Sometimes a great crisis may be the catalyst. Or it may be something from our childhood such as a piano recital, an academic contest or an athletic event. It may have been when we were a member of a team or an organization. The catalyst could have been your involvement in what you felt was some great cause. It may have been something simple but nevertheless made an impact on you.

Look back over your life and think of a time when you were at your very best — a time when you felt like you were fulfilling your potential and/or giving yourself to something that was bigger than you were — a time when you felt really alive. As you write, describe that experience in as much detail as possible.

_____

_____

_____

_____

_____

_____

_____

_____

_____

_____

_____

_____

_____

_____

_____

Your Very Best: Continued

Now record your answers to the following questions, again in as much detail as possible:

How did you feel?

_____

_____

_____

_____

What made it significant?

_____

_____

_____

_____

How did it impact others?

_____

_____

_____

_____

Chapter 4

That the Powerful Play Goes On

In the film *Dead Poet's Society* Robin Williams portrays an instructor in a private school charged with the daunting challenge of teaching teenage boys the value of poetry. In one poignant scene he huddles the entire class around him in the middle of his classroom and recites these lines penned by Walt Whitman: "*O me! O life... of the questions of these recurring; of the endless trains of the faithless — of cities filled with the foolish; what good amid these, O me, O life? Answer. That you are here — that life exists, and identity; that the powerful play goes on and you may contribute a verse.*"

Then, as he searches the eyes of the young men, he asks, "What will your verse be?"

Author Po Bronson was asking himself a similar question. It ended up becoming the title of one of his books, *What Should I Do With My Life?* It wasn't like Bronson hadn't been successful. He had already written three best sellers: *The Nudist on the Late Shift, The First $20 Million Is Always the Hardest* and *Bombardiers*.

He described his quest on his web site: "For answers, I crossed the landscape of America to find people who have struggled to unearth their true calling — people of all ages, from all classes, of every profession, who have found fulfillment; those who fought with the seduction of money, intensity, and novelty, but overcame their allure; those who broke away from the chorus to learn the sound of their own voice."

Are we merely mass produced clones in a chorus? Or does each individual possess a specific and unique voice? I agree with Shakespeare and Whitman. The world is a stage, life is a powerful play and we each have a role. The curtain was raised from the foundations of the world and each succeeding generation constitutes another act. New players continually appear to deliver their verses, and then exit to make way for others.

You were created with a singularly unique voice to deliver a specific verse in life's powerful play.

You Are Not a Clone

For most of our lives we hear purpose expressed in terms that define us as mere members of a chorus — that our purpose is to "serve God" or "to have relationship with God" or "to glorify God." So, how do we glorify God? Jesus revealed how he glorified God while praying just hours before his crucifixion, "I glorified you (God) on earth by completing down to the last detail what you assigned me to do." If that is how the Son of God glorified God then how do we glorify God? By completing down to the last detail what he assigned *us* to do.

When we are fulfilling our purpose — our assignment — we *are* glorifying God. So it's essential that we find out what that assignment is. According to the Avodah Institute, Avodah (Ah´-voe-dah) is a Hebrew word used in the Bible that has two distinct yet intertwined meanings — *worship* and *work*. What purer form of worship could there be than to be actively fulfilling God's purpose for our lives through our work?

If God has the hairs on our heads numbered and a fallen sparrow doesn't escape his notice, doesn't it seem logical that each individual must play an important role in an intricately designed plan? If not, life is just a cruel experiment — reducing the role of the human species to little more than laboratory animals navigating the maze of reward and punishment, seeking pleasure and avoiding pain.

There has to be a specific reason for my existence or I'm just an interchangeable part with anyone else. There has to be a reason for my uniqueness. If everyone's purpose is the same, then why didn't God just clone Adam?

In *The 6th Day*, Arnold Schwarzenegger plays the role of a helicopter pilot who survives a near-fatal accident and returns to his home — only to find that he's been replaced by an exact duplicate of himself, a clone.

I watched an interview with Arnie while he was out on the talk show circuit plugging *The 6th Day*. The host asked him if he would like to be cloned. "Yes," he replied. "Because I want to do so many things and if there were two of me I could accomplish so much more." I guess he was already thinking about becoming governor of California even then.

After successfully cloning animals, it was only a matter of time before someone started thinking about cloning humans. Of course, the issue of cloning brings with it some sobering moral and ethical questions. Cloning plants and livestock is one thing, but when we start thinking about cloning humans, we start wondering if man has gotten too big for his britches.

I don't think we have to worry about there being two Arnolds. In his book, *If I Knew Then What I Know Now,* Bill Bonnstetter contends that even if someone could recreate you physically, no one could clone the part of you that's really you:

> *Your mother's body chemistry would need to be the exact replica of when you were in the womb. Some research suggests that outside environment has an effect on the baby before birth, so this variable would have to be duplicated as well. After your entrance into the world, every interaction and relationship would have to occur at exactly at the identical point of time and each response would have to be repeated exactly — after all we are looking for the perfect match. You see, in order to duplicate you, we must replicate the billions of interactions you have throughout your life, which is absolutely impossible.*

There can't be two of you. If you can be positively identified by your fingerprint, the pattern of the blood vessels in the retina of your eye, the unique swagger of your walk and the

DNA taken from a single cell of a single strand of your hair doesn't it make sense that you were created for a singularly unique purpose?

Your Piece of the Puzzle

A play has many roles. Each is important. If each actor simply recited lines in the absence of the other actors the play wouldn't make sense. The actors would deliver disconnected, meaningless lectures. Each actor's lines are woven into the intricate tapestry of the entire story. Each role is different, yet each fulfills a purpose. Your roles may be multiple and varied but your purpose is singular and unique.

Imagine that you are a puzzle piece. By yourself what value do you have? Your uniqueness, devoid of the other pieces, renders you an ill-conceived object of abstract art. The fundamental principle of architectural design is *form follows function*. Your piece of the puzzle by itself has no function. That would make you *dysfunctional*. Dysfunctional people epitomize purposelessness.

What do you need to be functional? One, you need to be on purpose (delivering your verse) and two; you need to find how you fit with the other pieces in the big picture (the powerful play). The puzzle is only fully functional when all the pieces are in their proper place.

Maslow said that we have a need to give ourselves to something that is bigger than we are. We're all standing around with a puzzle piece in our hands subconsciously asking, "Where does my piece of the puzzle fit in life's big picture?" This is why so many people are not motivated in the workplace. They see no connection between their work and life's big picture. The result is to work as little as possible to earn as much as possible to quit working as soon as possible. The ultimate goal in life for most people is retirement. What's wrong with this picture? That's just it. There is no picture.

Have you noticed how many people today are involved in some type of activist group? These people willingly contribute thousands of dollars to these causes. They show up at rallies and protests, and pay their own way. Why? Because they want to give themselves to something bigger than they are. They aren't filling that need in their vocation so they look outside their work for a cause to give themselves to. They want their piece of the puzzle to count in life's big picture.

PPSS

In analyzing my own purpose and in helping others find and fulfill theirs, I've found four critical elements that are common to an individual's purpose. Your purpose is PPSS:

- It is **positive.** You were created to make a positive contribution to life's powerful play.

- It is **powerful.** Your purpose is part of something much bigger than you are. Your piece of the puzzle is critical.

- It is **simple**. It's a verse, not a dissertation.

- And most importantly your purpose has something to do with **serving** others. You were not put here on earth to be self-serving.

Humans are the only animals that can *choose* to serve. It is the unique attribute of our superhuman race. All other animals must be forced to serve. They serve only when manipulated by reward and punishment.

In the brilliant Italian film, *Life is Beautiful*, Guido, the lead character, has gone to work in the restaurant of a hotel owned by his uncle. In one comical yet poignant scene, the uncle is tutoring Guido on the finer points of being a waiter, "Serving is a supreme art," says the uncle. "God is the first servant."

If we are indeed created in God's image, then the most critical element of our purpose has to do with serving. Since serving is a supreme art it is a superhuman desire to serve others. The *only* way we can serve God is by serving others.

"I don't know what your mission in life is," said Albert Schweitzer, "but you'll only find true happiness by serving others." In some form or fashion, everyone's purpose has to do with serving. It can be as altruistic as Mother Teresa caring for the sick and dying in the streets of Calcutta or as capitalistic as Sam Walton building the world's largest retailing empire on the simple philosophy of 100% customer satisfaction. Serving will bring you happiness. Serving will bring you success.

Your Superhuman Is A Servant

All of the superheroes in literature are selfless, tireless servants. They expect nothing in return for their noble acts. They are motivated not by reward and punishment but by the fulfillment of their purpose. They understand who they are in life's big picture. Their service to others is a supreme art. That is why they are super. Super and supreme share this common definition in the dictionary — superiority over all others.

Your animal body *survives* by responding to legitimate needs and fears. The superhuman *thrives* by responding to the call of purpose. Your superhuman is *supreme* or *superior* because it is created in God's image, a perfect *reflection* of its Creator.

Let me stress *simple*. Too often people think of their purpose in terms of being a *mission statement*. The problem with this is the same problem with most organizations' mission statements. They are so long and convoluted that any meaning they might possess is lost in the verbiage. And as I tell consulting clients, if no one can tell you what the mission is, there is no mission. People who have crafted personal mission statements have done just that — they've *crafted* them. Your purpose isn't something you craft or conjure up. It's something you already possess so you simply uncover it through a process of self-discovery.

I've stopped using the term *mission* because people automatically try to *craft* their purpose using mission statement terminology. Your purpose is not a page-long diatribe. Most mission statements are filled with *whats* and *hows*. Your purpose is the *why* behind the *whats* and *hows*. The *whats* and the *hows* are roles and vehicles which I'll discuss in the next chapter. And you don't *define* your purpose, you *find* your purpose. It has already been defined for you by God. It's the reason *you were created* — your reason for *being*. It's your *verse* — not the whole play.

The Quantum Leap

Chad came to one of our workshops armed with a personal mission statement. It was a page-long, typewritten, mini-constitution in 8-point type developed from the many self-development seminars he had attended. In spite of all this verbiage, he was still searching for his purpose.

Chad is a strapping, 6'8" tall man's man who played football at the University of Tulsa and likes to hunt and fish. He wanted to know his purpose and he wanted to know it *now*. If discovering one's purpose was a matter of physical force, Chad would have squeezed it out of himself, or somebody else, a long time ago.

We often invite past participants to come to our workshops and share how they discovered their purpose and the impact it has made in their lives. In the workshop Chad attended, one of our past participants shared her story. She concluded her brief testimonial with, "My purpose is to *shine the light*."

This, as I learned later, made Chad mad. "Here was this woman standing up there telling me that her purpose was to *shine the light*," he told me. "It wasn't fair. Her purpose was only three words. I had 3,000 words but no purpose." But that was a catalyst that helped Chad make a quantum leap in the purpose process. After the workshop he described this to me in scientific terms. Although I knew our process worked I didn't know *how* it worked. His description made sense to me so I asked him to write it down. Here's *Dr. Chad's Quantum Physics of Purpose*:

> *Quantum physics looks at the incredibly small relationships within and around the atom. Most of us have looked in some form or fashion at what is termed Newtonian Physics which deals with the study of such things as the way that matter interacts with other matter, i.e. velocity, gravity, etc. It can describe the order of planets or the energy exchange that occurs during a car accident or a game of pool.*

> *Quantum physics on the other hand goes much smaller and describes the interactions of electrons, how they surround the nucleus and other subatomic actions. It looks at the electrons, protons and neutrons and takes into account that the rules of regular physics change dramatically when we reduce to the subatomic level. This is where the purpose workshop fits in. Hang on to find out how.*

43

Quantum physics describes the particles that make up the subatomic particles. It gets real small real quick. The electrons don't really orbit the nucleus like planets; they are really like blurred probabilities around it. Protons and neutrons are really made of three quarks each with a flavor and one of three colors. Oh, and let's not forget the gluons (what a great name!) that act as glue to hold the whole mess together.

All this craziness was started with the idea of the quanta. A quanta is the smallest amount of energy that an electron can give off or absorb when a change of energy level occurs. This is where it relates back to the concept of orbiting planets. To get from one level to the next or back to the original level, an amount of energy is given off or absorbed by the orbiting electrons. It also can be related to stories in a building. A person cannot get off the elevator between the third and fourth floors. You have to either get off on the third or the fourth. When a person does get off there is a certain amount of weight and space or energy that is either given up or received. When electrons exchange levels or blurred probabilities of levels in their relationship to the nucleus they give off a whole number of quantas.

The concept to grasp here is that it takes a certain amount of energy to be used or given off to get to or from a certain level and it can only be a whole number amount.

Some of us try, in our search for purpose, to give a little effort towards finding our purpose. At the purpose workshop one of the things that become evident is when people start reaching their supernatural level of purposeful revelation. We hear things like, "I just found my purpose. I got it" or "Wow, I have known that all the time, but I just now connected with it." These are supernatural moments where the quanta level of understanding is given off or received and the perfect fit is established for revelation of your purpose. These people have just made a "quantum leap" from searching for their purpose to having it revealed to them by God. Their purpose had been out there the whole time in a level of "blurred probabilities." They have just released the just-right "quanta" amount of energy for it to be revealed.

I can't improve on that. It's impossible to predict exactly how or when someone receives the revelation. The main thing to keep in mind is not to worry about it but stay engaged in the process. Your purpose might be revealed to you at anytime while you are reading this book or completing one of the exercises. It may happen after reading chapter one or three weeks after you've finished the book. It may come to you while you're jogging. That's when my wife, Sondra, discovered her purpose. It came to her one day while jogging on her mini-trampoline and listening to a Leo Buscalia tape on her walkman.

We have people who discover their purpose at different times during our workshops and some who discover it after the workshop. One of our participants, Trisha, left frustrated only to discover her purpose two weeks later on a flight home from a vacation. As she looked out the window at the wing of the plane, the words of a popular song came to mind:

It hit me as we were landing at DFW — "wind beneath the wings." My purpose is to be the wind beneath the wings of people I love. Whether it be my sister campaigning for her husband or my friend who is beginning a new business or Ike (Trisha's husband); I want to be their invisible support that helps them to "fly." I was very reluctant to tell my friends because I was afraid they would laugh or think it was very corny. But when I finally told them they all agreed that this was without a doubt my purpose and even gave me other examples of how I have always been doing it.

A couple of weeks after attending one of our workshops, Debbie wrote to tell me of a dream she had:

I had a wild dream last night and the phrase that kept going over and over in my mind throughout that dream was, "help others find their dream." I don't know if this is my purpose or not and I don't know where to go from here, but I'm wondering if this is my purpose I've been looking for.

I know that I have a great desire to help people find out what they want to be or what direction they want to go in life. I am particularly interested in helping high school students find out what direction they want to go in. It angers me that there are not more programs in high school that help those students with career choices. Many of them do not go on to college because they don't know what they want to do so they do what is familiar to them — continue their career with the part-time job they have had through high school or go to work doing something their parents are doing or whatever.

So, maybe this is a passion I should explore — just don't know where to start. Anyway, I thought I would share this with you. You said that "it would just come to you one day" and this one came in a dream.

Debbie experienced the quantum leap in a dream. When you are searching for your purpose be prepared. It's like Candid Camera — don't be surprised if sometime, somewhere, someplace when you least expect it, God steps up to you and says, "Smile! This is *your* purpose!"

Kirbyjon Caldwell graduated from the prestigious Wharton School of Business at the University of Pennsylvania with an MBA. He did a stint on Wall Street then returned to his native Houston to work for a bond firm. But the path of God's purpose included a supernatural detour. He quit his job and enrolled in seminary. His first assignment after graduation was a church with 25 members in a middle-class black neighborhood in Houston. Today it has over 10,000 members.

But that's just part of the story. Using his financial expertise he founded the Power Center, which pumps $30 million into Houston's economy each year and employs nearly 300 people. The Power Center includes a small business center, a private school, a technology center, a hospital clinic and a bank.

"They say there are two great moments in your life," says Caldwell. "When you are born and then when you know why you are born." What's it like when you know *why* you were born? He described it like this, "It was like an eclipse, when your mind, psyche, soul and spirit line up in perfect harmony with God's primary purpose for your being."

Sounds like the Quantum Physics of Purpose to me.

"Why" Instead of "What and How"

My purpose is to help people reach their full potential. That's my singular *why* — my verse in life's powerful play. I play multiple roles including writer, speaker and consultant to deliver my verse.

This exercise will help you understand what *your* purpose might look like by considering what the purpose of some notable people might be. To the best of your ability identify the purpose for each of the following people and write it down. Think in terms of a singular *why* instead of terms of multiple *whats* and/or *hows*. Don't write long verbose mission statements. Instead, write one brief sentence that incorporates the four critical elements of purpose — it should be Positive, Powerful, Simple and Serving.

Martin Luther King, Jr.

_____

_____

Mother Teresa

_____

_____

Albert Einstein

_____

_____

Bill Gates

_____

_____

Oprah Winfrey

_____

_____

I've written what I think the purpose for each of these people might be. This is just my opinion of course, but to check out what I came up with go to page 122. No peeking until you've written your answers!

Chapter 5

What's My Line?

What's My Line? was a popular television game show in the 1950s and 60s. Contestants with unusual occupations would join the host on stage while a panel tried to guess his or her vocation by way of a good natured and often humorous interrogation. My favorite part of the program was the final guest, who was always a celebrity. Since the celebrity guest would be readily recognized, the panel donned masks that kept them "in the dark" so to speak. The celebrity guest would disguise his or her voice to throw the panel while answering the questions. It made for a lot of laughs.

As children we play our own little version of *What's My Line?* — except we are asking *ourselves* the questions and trying to guess what our occupation *should* be. We fantasize about what we *want* to be when we grow up. As we grow older we are told that to be successful and happy we need to go to school and make good grades so we can go to college and make good grades so we can go get a good job. Why? So that we can make money, have a nice home, nice clothes, nice cars, take vacations, put our kids through college and retire in comfort. So we follow the formula, get a good job and guess what?

Our *line* of work often turns out to just be work.

I was listening to the radio one New Years Eve when the host of the program asked listeners to go to the station's website and complete this sentence: "As I look back on the past year, I am..." You were given the following options:

a)   Content in my life and job.
b)   Content in my job, but not my life.
c)   Content in my life, but not my job.
d)   Don't have a job or a life.

I logged onto the station's web site to find out how people responded. Here are the results on a percentage basis:

a)   Content in my life and job. (31%)
b)   Content in my job, but not my life. (4%)
c)   Content in my life, but not my job. (60%).
d)   Don't have a job or a life. (3%)

I particularly liked the last response.

Notice that nearly 70% of the respondents *were not* content with their life *and* their job. The results of this unscientific poll were nearly a mirror image of the findings in the Life@Work survey I shared earlier. It once again validates the fact that people are quietly desperate.

Turn to the help wanted section of the classifieds in any Sunday newspaper and you'll find more ads for positions in health care than any other industry. Are they creating that many new jobs in health care? No. So what's going on? People are going back and forth, from hospital to hospital, clinic to clinic and medical practice to medical practice. Is it for more money? Better benefits? More vacation time?

Let's face it, every industry has a fairly standardized pay scale and benefits package within a geographic region. So that typically isn't the reason for turnover. Healthcare workers are subconsciously saying, "I'm looking for more than a paycheck and pension. I went into health care for altruistic reasons and I know there has to be *someplace* out there where I can find happiness and fulfillment in my work. So I'll keep looking until I find it." Translation: "My animal is being fed but my superhuman is going hungry. I see no purpose in my work so I'm trying to make as much money as I can Monday through Friday so I can spend it on something I enjoy this weekend to distract me from the fact that I have to go back to the salt mines Monday morning."

When we are working only for money and what it will buy we are no different than an animal seeking food, shelter and safety. Unfortunately, this is why most of the workforce today is not motivated. We're just animals manipulated by reward and punishment. And more money isn't the answer. "I need more money" most often can be translated as: "Look, I hate my job, but I can be bribed. Give me more money and I'll keep my mouth shut, keep my nose clean and do as I'm told." Then what happens?

Six months later I want another raise. The pain of my work is once again greater than the pleasure of the reward. I need more stimulation. Doing my best Jerry McGuire imitation I say, "Show me the money!" This is a never-ending cycle — because money *never* was the real issue. But since I've been conditioned to respond to reward and punishment, I don't consciously understand what the real issue is — a lack of purpose.

After a steady dose of workplace reality, we often find ourselves right back where we started as children, asking ourselves what we want to be when we grow up. The problem is we *are* grown up. So we change jobs and what happens? Same song, second verse. It reminds me of a scene from the movie *As Good As It Gets*. Jack Nicholson plays an obsessive-compulsive writer who is in perpetual therapy. One day as he walks out of the office of his therapist, he looks around at the other people waiting to see the psychologist and asks aloud, "Do you ever wonder, is this as good as it gets?"

As part of his research for *What Should I Do With My Life?* Po Bronson interviewed a woman who kept referring to it as his *What Do I Want to Be When I Grow Up?* book. "I think that's a notably different question," writes Bronson. "It lacks the 'Should,' which hints at a moral or aspirational imperative, and it overemphasizes 'Want,' as in *I want I want I want...* Our wants are fleeting. They are also indulgent. Every philosophy draws a hard line between what you want and what you need."

If you have children you hear "I want" a lot. You hate to tell them no, but you know what they think they want isn't anywhere close to what they really want. It's like the scene from

Bruce Almighty, where Bruce (Jim Carrey) is given a chance by God (Morgan Freeman) to play God. Bruce causes big problems when he answers people's prayers.

> *Bruce: I just gave them all what they wanted.*
> *God: Yeah, but since when does anyone have a clue about what they want?*

"What do you want?" isn't the right question. The right question is, "What is your *purpose*." It's the *form* follows *function* follows *purpose* thing again. We get it backwards. We are searching for the form instead of searching for the purpose.

Planes, Trains & Automobiles

The "What do you want to be when you grow up?" question has conditioned us to think of our life's purpose in terms of a vocation. When we were children we might say, "I want to be a teacher, a doctor, an astronaut or maybe even President of the United States." Unfortunately this carries over into adulthood. We confuse our purpose with a vocation. Think of it like this. Your purpose is your destination in life. A vocation is merely a vehicle that takes you there.

For example, my vehicles are speaking, writing and consulting. Another way to think of it is that these are the roles I play to deliver my verse in life's powerful play. All of them are effective vehicles to fulfill my purpose of helping people reach their full potential. But what if I *defined* my purpose as being a professional speaker or a consultant? Well, you wouldn't be reading this right now. Writing is also an effective vehicle for me to fulfill my purpose.

A four-wheel drive SUV and a sports car are both vehicles. One can crawl over rough terrain, the other zips down the freeway. Both are forms of transportation that perform different functions. Both will serve the purpose of getting you to your destination. You don't drive the same car forever. Believe me, I've tried. It's the same with the vehicles that carry you on the road to your purpose. For example, you might be a schoolteacher and later become a newspaper reporter. Both can perform the function of educating. Both are good vehicles — but for what purpose?

When we don't know our destination (purpose) in life, it's like driving down the interstate looking for the right exit. We take an exit and drive around awhile until we finally throw up our hands and say, "This isn't it." So we get back on the interstate and drive to the next exit for some more accidental tourism. All of us have experienced the frustration of being lost. Doesn't it make more sense to just stop and ask for directions?

We can't look for vehicles with no earthly idea of *where* or *why* we're going in the first place. In *Planes, Trains and Automobiles* Steve Martin and John Candy are trying to get home to Chicago in time for Thanksgiving. Their journey is a comedy of errors that requires them to engage multiple modes of transportation. They didn't care *how* they got to Chicago as long as they got there. We too, need to know the destination first. It is only then that we can determine what vehicles we need to get us there. Like Steve Martin and John Candy, we might use several. It was only after I found my purpose that I found the right vehicles to fulfill it.

The discovery of your purpose may put you in the market for a new vehicle. When Dan showed up at one of our workshops he was a quietly desperate attorney on the road *most* traveled. He had "followed the formula" but discovered his "law" vehicle had turned out to just be work. About eighteen months after Dan attended our workshop I had lunch with him and he shared how the discovery of his purpose had transformed his life:

When I graduated from college I had no plans and no idea what I wanted to do with my life. I had always just taken the next natural step automatically; graduate from high school — go to college — graduate from college — get a job. I didn't really want to go to law school, but I had been offered a scholarship and graduated with honors.

The next natural step after graduating from law school is to get a job at a law firm. So that's what I did. I didn't have the passion to really dive into the work and learn more about it, and excel, and I could only go so far on self-discipline. I began to grow very frustrated with the emptiness I felt towards my job.

One day, I was meeting in my office with a young couple who were going through a divorce. As they discussed the terms of the divorce I couldn't get this thought out of my mind, "I think this marriage can be saved. I would much rather be working to save this marriage than helping them with the divorce." That was the first day that I ever considered being a counselor. The more I thought about it, the more excited I became.

I attended the purpose workshop and a common theme continued to surface. I realized that my purpose is to "resolve conflicts and bring unity."

Eventually I left the firm. But I wasn't ready to take the leap of faith necessary to really dive into my purpose. I started a window washing business then went back to work at another law firm. Within a month, I knew I was in the wrong place. I was miserable. I decided to quit my job and go to school for a master's degree in counseling.

I gave my boss a full month's advance notice. A couple of weeks later, he came into my office and told me, "Dan, usually when somebody quits a job, their work begins to decline. But since you quit, you have become more effective, more productive, more confident. It's like somebody took the old Dan and replaced him with a new one. I have never seen anything like this. It's been a learning experience for me watching this change in you." I left with his blessing because he could clearly see the life-giving effect of me discovering my purpose.

The effect was almost immediate. I felt like life was pouring into me. I felt like I had been asleep for a very long time and now I was awake and anxious to get started.

Before I started taking my classes, I went to Africa for 10 weeks to work with a friend of mine with World Relief. After I had been there a few weeks he told me, "When you first told me that you were thinking about becoming a counselor, I couldn't see it. But now I can see it's a good fit."

All he had ever known me to be was a guy who was trying to fit a lawyer/business man mold, and a person who generally lacked passion. It was especially rewarding to me to have him say that I was definitely more optimistic and positive than he had ever known me to be.

When Dan found his purpose, it set him on the right road. He found that being an attorney wasn't the right *vehicle* for him to "resolve conflicts and bring unity." So he changed vehicles. As his friend observed, being a counselor looked like a good fit for Dan.

A Perfect Fit

As a young actor, Michael Caine was struggling to make a living. One day while in the waiting room of a casting agency, the owner asked him for his coat size and inseam length. Caine told him that he wore a size 40 jacket and his inseam measured 32 inches. The casting agent waved him into his office and told him he would be playing a policeman in a small film the next day. He was selected solely because the wardrobe company's policeman's uniform matched his measurements. Michael Caine got the job because he was "a perfect fit" for the role.

When Arnold Schwarzenegger first showed up in Hollywood, the experts said he'd never make it. His name was too long, his accent was too thick and he didn't have the right build. At the time he just wasn't the prototype of a leading man by Hollywood's standards. So what happened? Arnold became a box office money machine. It turns out that his accent is just right, his build is perfect and nobody has a problem pronouncing Schwarzenegger. Arnold created the new prototype for Hollywood's leading man.

A half century before Arnold made the scene, the screen test assessment of another Hollywood hopeful sounded dismal: "Slightly bald, can't sing, can dance a little." They were right — he was slightly bald and he couldn't sing — but Fred Astaire could dance more than just a little.

I can remember when Elvis Presley first appeared on television in the 1950s. His leg started shaking and teenagers went wild (parents went crazy). He didn't just sing — he gyrated. Elvis knew he was no world-beater as a singer — but he understood what made him unique. "I'm not fooling anybody," he said. "My voice is ordinary. If I stood still when I sing I might as well go back to driving a truck."

Arnold, Fred and Elvis were all very different but each successfully capitalized on their uniqueness. Successful people in any field of endeavor capitalize on their uniqueness.

One day while driving down the road I tuned in to catch Paul Harvey's news program on the radio. For some reason Sam Donaldson was filling in for Paul Harvey. Sam was reading the same script but it just didn't have that unique Paul Harvey flavor. Paul Harvey can not only turn a phrase, he can turn a phrase into an adventure. He keeps you hanging on every twist and turn of his verbal adventure until he bids you ado with, "This is Paul Harvey … good day!"

Having Sam Donaldson fill in for Paul Harvey is like having a bulldog fill in for a collie. Sam Donaldson has made his mark keeping politicians at bay in front of a camera. Listening to Paul Harvey on the radio is kind of like a visit with a member of the family on the phone. Sam Donaldson can't be Paul Harvey and Paul Harvey can't be Sam Donaldson. Each has a unique behavioral style that makes them a perfect fit for their respective vehicles.

You, too, have a unique behavioral profile that makes you a perfect fit for specific roles to deliver your verse in life's powerful play. Ninety-nine percent of the genetic code mapped on the twenty-three chromosomes in each of our cells is the same in all humans. But it is that one percent difference in our DNA that embodies our singular uniqueness. That difference is exhibited in our natural behavior pattern that makes us a perfect fit for specific vehicles and enables us to play different roles.

We use a variety of computer generated assessments that reveal how people are behaviorally equipped to fulfill their purpose. It gives them insight as to what vehicles might best serve their purpose. To help you determine how you're equipped to fulfill your purpose I've included a simple assessment for you to complete at the end of this chapter. None of us are "purebreds." We are much too individualistic to be put in a box with one label on it but we can broadly categorize behavior into four basic styles. We could call these styles anything but I like to think of them as bulldogs, coyotes, shepherds and pointers.

- **Bulldogs** are known for their tenacity. "The nose of the bulldog is slanted backwards," said Winston Churchill, "so that it can breathe without letting go." If there was ever a bulldog it was Churchill who once delivered a commencement address using only seven words, "Never give up. Never, never give up."
- **Coyotes** are wild dogs that are able to adapt to a wide variety of habitats. They are very vocal creatures that like to howl when the sun goes down. In fact, their scientific name, Canis latrans, means "barking dog."
- **Shepherds** can be one of several breeds of that belong to a group of dogs classified as herders. The American Kennel Club points out that while many of these dogs may never cross paths with a farm animal their nurturing instinct makes them great companions that gently herd their owners, especially children.
- **Pointers** are hard-working birddogs with a single-minded focus. They find birds and *point,* coming to a frozen standstill. They retrieve your bird after you shoot it, then it's back to finding and pointing.

There are 4 Ps of behavior that help determine which of the four styles you most identify with — how you deal with problems, people, pace and procedures:

- When faced with a **problem** are you aggressive in solving it or more methodical and analytical?
- Do you verbally influence **people** or do you prefer to use facts and figures?
- Do you prefer a predictable, steady **pace** or do you like a lot of variety and change?
- When it comes to policies and **procedures** do you do things by the book or do you see lots of options?

Let's take a look at my behavior when it comes to the 4 Ps:

- **Problems** – I never saw a problem I didn't like. Give me a problem and I won't quit until it's solved. I like big challenges. This quality has served me well. I would have never survived that first six months in that run-down old farmhouse if it hadn't been for my bulldog-like tenacity.

- **People** – I am a verbal influencer. It's a coyote trait but I do my howling in front of an audience and not at the moon. I get paid to talk as a speaker and consultant. I use my verbal skills to sell myself and our services. And even though writing is nonverbal communication I have a *conversational* writing style. Know what I mean?

- **Pace** – I like a lot of variety. I live by the philosophy of "if it ain't broke, break it." It's another coyote trait. Coyotes are among the most curious of animals. I like to explore. Change doesn't happen to me, I make it happen. I work a varied schedule and juggle a lot of balls. And when consulting with clients, I am either being a catalyst for change or helping them adapt to change.

- **Procedures** – My computer generated profile describes my approach to procedures like this: "Jim doesn't mind following the rules as long as he gets to make the rules." This is probably one part bulldog and one part coyote. As far as I'm concerned, there is more than one way to skin a cat and I've skinned a lot of cats trying to figure out every one of them. I see lots of options. As you have probably figured out by now, I definitely color outside the lines.

Speaking, writing and consulting come naturally to me because of the behavioral characteristics I just described. This is my *natural* behavioral style. It's natural because I was created with that style. And because it's natural I'm really good at what I do. No brag, just fact. I can relate to something the legendary Ray Charles said when asked about how he learned to communicate his feelings through song, "It's natural, babe. I wouldn't know how to tell somebody else how to do it, and I wouldn't know how to stop it in myself."

Michael Jordan was a natural at basketball. But remember what happened when he tried his hand at baseball? He never made it out of the minor leagues. Likewise, I would be a colossal failure, let's say, at nuclear physics. As an animal science major I was required to take classes in chemistry, organic chemistry, biology, physiology and physics. My first two years were the same as pre-med. I found myself in classrooms filled with students who were trying to get into medical or veterinary school and they were the ones setting the curve on the grading scale.

It wasn't a fair fight.

I graduated with a 3.0000015 grade point average — definitely not at the top of my class. But because I color outside the lines I've been able to capitalize on my degree in animal science and agricultural background.

You won't find many management consultants with animal science degrees. My education, coupled with my work with livestock, has given me a unique perspective of human behavior that led me to many of the conclusions I'm sharing with you in this book.

I had no idea when I was punching cows or selling cow chow that I would end up doing what I am today. But God did. He equipped me perfectly to fulfill my purpose of helping people reach their full potential. He gave me a creative mind to come up with solutions to problems when I consult. He gave me the ability to paint pictures in the minds of my audiences and my readers. He gave me the passion of a poet, the persuasion of a salesman and the perseverance of a bulldog. These attributes are perfectly tailored for the vehicles of consulting, writing and speaking.

Now, let's see how my wife, Sondra, is uniquely equipped when it comes to the 4 Ps:

- **Problems** – She has an analytical approach to solving problems and facing challenges. Much of the time, she thinks that "time will take care of it." Because Sondra believes people have the solutions for their problems within themselves, she seldom "pushes" people but helps them reach the right conclusions on their own and on their own time schedule. This is a shepherd trait.

- **People** – Sondra can be verbal when the situation calls for it but also uses information, facts and data to influence people. She's comfortable in a supporting role and doesn't need to be the center of attention. It is sometimes difficult for her to be in the position of being the "up front" person. But a good shepherd works from behind not in front.

- **Pace** – She is punctual, patient and tolerant. Another pointer/shepherd trait. Sondra does routine a lot better than I do. She's more interested in relationships while I'm more interested in results. Relationships require a slower, more methodical pace — a shepherd trait. She likes to know what is expected of her and then she'll work hard to fulfill those expectations.

- **Procedure** – She usually believes rules are rules and you're not supposed to break the rules. If the flashing light says "DO NOT WALK" you do not walk — even if there isn't a car within 50 miles of the intersection. For this reason, we've spent most of our married lives with me halfway across the street while she's still standing on the curb waiting for the light to change. This is definitely the pointer in her — stay on task and don't deviate.

Sondra's purpose is "to set the captive free." And her natural behavioral pattern serves her well. All of us carry a lot of old baggage that tends to hold us captive. Couple her natural behavioral style with her training in psychology and she's perfectly equipped to help people rid themselves of the baggage that holds them back from reaching their potential.

Sondra and I each bring a different piece of the puzzle to our partnership and our marriage. Both of our pieces of the puzzle fit together perfectly. She has strengths where I have weaknesses and vice versa.

Roles, Goals & Vehicles

People confuse roles, goals and vehicles with their purpose. That's why Chad had a 3,000 word mission statement. It included a lot of roles, goals and vehicles. It was *well* meaning but didn't have *much* meaning. Aretha Franklin, the "Queen of Soul" knows music is not the destination but merely a means to an end, "This is a vehicle for my creative expression and I enjoy bringing happiness to others." Bringing happiness to others is the end, while music is the means.

Vehicles are not just vocations — they can be other roles we play in life. We have had some people who have come to our workshop believing their purpose *was* to be a mother or a father. Those are critical roles but we only actively play those roles for part of our lives. We play many roles — husband, wife, father, mother, son, daughter.

We have vocations and avocations. We may do volunteer work. All of these can be vehicles. How many can you have? Who knows? It's not important. What is important is to find our purpose and focus our energy on fulfilling it. When I did that I discovered the vehicles *came to me*. I know — that's not natural. You're right, it's supernatural. Of course you have a choice when presented with a vehicle. You can kick the tires and give it the once over or you can crawl behind the wheel, turn the key and take it for a spin. You may not know exactly where it will take you. Consider John's story:

> When I came to the workshop, wearing skepticism and doubt like an unholy toga, I was a very unhappy computer technician. I knew that I was missing out on something but I didn't know what.
>
> I found my purpose on my first day and I knew that I was supposed to "Connect with People and Ignite Their hearts."
>
> It was interesting that during the conference I found that I had always been gifted as a writer, speaker, actor and singer. All of these vehicles are ways for me to connect with people's hearts and to ignite them.
>
> Since then I have been in five different commercials and a national trailer that will show nationwide this year in over 800 theatres.
>
> I now work for a video production company as a creative writer. I also produce many of our projects as well.
>
> I will perform live in front of 13,000 people next year. My writing is now in front of thousands and I am now in the best place ever to get my book out.

I can't tell you how many people I know are struggling in their life trying to find some meaning in the everyday mundane. I find that it has so impacted me that it filters its way into everything that I write. Movies where the hero discovers their true potential now leap out at me.

I received the above letter from John a year after he attended our workshop. He discovered his purpose and his superhuman was liberated. He was riding in the vehicle of an unhappy computer technician and now has a fleet of vehicles that include acting, directing, producing, writing and speaking. This is how the transformational power of purpose works.

It isn't natural, it's supernatural.

We also have people come to our workshops and after finding their purpose discover they are already in vehicles that are perfect fits for them. But now they *know.* They aren't continually asking themselves, "Is this what I'm supposed to be doing in life?"

Red Skelton played many roles in life. He starred in vaudeville, radio, movies and television. But it was in television where he left his most indelible impression. He created and played an array of unforgettable characters on his program like Clem Kadiddlehopper and Freddy the Freeloader.

Red ran away from home at the tender age of ten to join a traveling medicine show: "Mom used to say I didn't run away from home; my destiny just caught up with me at an early age." While he played many roles in many mediums of the entertainment industry he never confused his roles, goals or vehicles with his purpose. Red Skelton knew exactly why he was put on planet earth. "If I can make people laugh," he said, "then I have served my purpose for God."

The thing I always liked about Red Skelton was that he seemed to be having as much fun during his performance as the audience. He laughed and he made us laugh. That's the wonderful thing about being on purpose. Like Ray Charles says, "It's natural babe." It's supernaturally natural. It flows, it's fun and it's fulfilling. Serving others, ironically, is self-serving. In the words of William H. Danforth, the founder of the Ralston Purina Company, "You give your life away and behold! A richer life comes back to you."

At the conclusion of his television program, Red Skelton signed off with his trademark, "Good night and God bless." He did indeed serve his purpose for God. And God certainly did bless. He blessed us with Red Skelton.

A Perfect Fit for You

What's your basic style? While this is not intended to be an in-depth analysis, you can get a good idea of your basic style by completing the inventory below. Check the box by each word that describes you. Choose any word that feels "right." In other words, don't think too hard. First responses are usually best.

	I	II	III	IV
Accurate				☐
Action Oriented	☐			
Activity Oriented				☐
Adaptable			☐	
Ambitious		☐		
Bold	☐			
Calm			☐	
Cautious				☐
Competitive	☐			
Conscientious				☐
Consistent				☐
Controlling	☐			
Cooperative			☐	
Creative		☐		
Detailed				☐
Dry Humor			☐	
Energetic		☐		
Enjoys Change		☐		
Enjoys Harmony			☐	
Enjoys Instructions				☐
Enjoys Routine			☐	
Enthusiastic		☐		
Excitable		☐		
Factual				☐
Firm	☐			
Friendly		☐		
Fun-loving		☐		
Goal Driven	☐			
Good Listener			☐	
Group Oriented		☐		
Impersonal				☐
Independent	☐			
Industrious	☐			
Inquisitive				☐
Inspirational		☐		
Initiator		☐		

	I	II	III	IV
Intuitive		☐		
Judges Quickly	☐			
Likes Variety		☐		
Logical				☐
Loyal			☐	
Mixes Easily		☐		
Non-demanding			☐	
Nurturing			☐	
Optimistic		☐		
Orderly				☐
Organized				☐
Patient			☐	
Perfectionistic				☐
Persistent	☐			
Personal			☐	
Precise				☐
Problem Solver	☐			
Productive	☐			
Promotes		☐		
Purposeful	☐			
Relational			☐	
Reserved				☐
Respectful			☐	
Scheduled				☐
Seeks Power	☐			
Self-reliant	☐			
Sensitive Feelings			☐	
Serious	☐			
Spontaneous		☐		
Strong Willed	☐			
Sympathetic			☐	
Takes Charge	☐			
Takes Risks		☐		
Technical Oriented				☐
Thoughtful			☐	
Tolerant			☐	

A Perfect Fit for You: Continued

To score, count the number of boxes you chose in each column (I, II, III or IV) and write that number in the spaces below.

I_____ **II**_____ **III**_____ **IV**_____

Your highest total determines your basic style. I = BULLDOG, II = COYOTE, III = SHEPHERD and IV = POINTER. Remember, no one is a purebred. Everyone is a hybrid or composite. On the next page are some of the behavioral traits of each of the basic styles. Put a check mark by the traits you believe most accurately describe you under each category. You should find that you possess the most traits associated with the highest totals from your assessments. So, if your basic style was II (COYOTE) you'll probably find a high number of your traits in that category. But don't neglect to list traits from other categories if you feel they apply.

Now, imagine that an organization wants to hire you and create the perfect job for you based on your unique qualifications. Rather than using your educational background and work experience however, use the behavioral traits you checked to write a brief résumé that you think would accurately describe the strengths you would bring to the job, your value to the team (organization), and the ideal environment for you to work in. Don't shortchange yourself. Make yourself look good!

_____

_____

_____

_____

_____

_____

_____

_____

_____

_____

A Perfect Fit for You: Continued

BULLDOGS

Strengths	Value to a Team	Ideal Work Environment
☐ Adventurous ☐ Competitive ☐ Daring ☐ Decisive ☐ Direct ☐ Innovative ☐ Persistent ☐ Problem Solver ☐ Results-oriented ☐ Self-starter	☐ Bottom line organizer ☐ Big picture visionary ☐ Challenges status quo ☐ Initiates activity ☐ Innovative	☐ Freedom from controls, supervision and details ☐ An innovative and futuristic-oriented environment ☐ Forum to express ideas and viewpoints ☐ Non-routine work ☐ Challenges and opportunities

COYOTES

Strengths	Value to a Team	Ideal Work Environment
☐ Charming ☐ Confident ☐ Convincing ☐ Enthusiastic ☐ Inspiring ☐ Optimistic ☐ Persuasive ☐ Popular ☐ Sociable ☐ Trusting	☐ Optimism ☐ Enthusiasm ☐ Creative problem solver ☐ Encourages others ☐ Team player ☐ Negotiates conflicts	☐ Lots of contact with people ☐ Freedom from control and detail ☐ Freedom of movement ☐ Forum for ideas to be heard ☐ Approachable supervisor with whom he can relate

SHEPHERDS

Strengths	Value to a Team	Ideal Work Environment
☐ Amiable ☐ Friendly ☐ Good listener ☐ Patient ☐ Relaxed ☐ Sincere ☐ Stable ☐ Steady ☐ Team Player ☐ Understanding	☐ Dependable team player ☐ Work for a leader and a cause ☐ Patient and empathetic ☐ Logical step-wise thinker ☐ Service-oriented	☐ Stable and predictable ☐ Environment that allows time to change ☐ Long-term work relationships ☐ Little conflict ☐ Freedom from restrictive rules

POINTERS

Strengths	Value to a Team	Ideal Work Environment
☐ Accurate ☐ Analytical ☐ Conscientious ☐ Courteous ☐ Diplomatic ☐ Fact-finder ☐ High standards ☐ Mature ☐ Patient ☐ Precise	☐ Maintain high standards ☐ Conscientious and steady ☐ Defines, clarifies, gets information and tests ☐ Comprehensive problem solver	☐ Need for critical thinking ☐ Technical or specialized work ☐ Close relationships with a small group ☐ Familiarity ☐ Private work area

A Perfect Fit for You: Continued

Based on the traits you checked on page 61 and your résumé, what type of vehicle or vehicles (vocations) do you think might be a good fit for you?

_____

_____

_____

_____

_____

Are you involved in activities (career, volunteer work, home, church, committees, etc.) at this time that are good vehicles for your behavioral profile? If not, can you think of any that might be?

_____

_____

_____

_____

_____

This exercise was designed to provide another piece to your purpose puzzle. While it gives you a quick snapshot of how you're behaviorally equipped to fulfill your purpose we have computer-generated career development assessments that can provide much more detailed information. We also provide career coaching. To learn more go to www.WhittEnterprises.com.

_____

_____

_____

_____

_____

Chapter 6

What You See Is What You Get

In our reward and punishment culture, success is most often defined by achievement, competence and recognition — the esteem needs on Maslow's hierarchy. With that as the standard, you are deemed successful by how much money you make, how smart you are, how beautiful you may be or how famous you become. It's a culture where celebrity rules. It's a recipe for an emotional breakdown because trying to succeed by those standards will leave most of us feeling like we're not quite up to snuff. In the words of Madonna, "I'm telling you that fame and fortune are not what they're cracked up to be. We live in a society that seems to value only physical things, only ephemeral things."

Al Franken's character on *Saturday Night Live*, Stuart Smalley, constantly reinforced his fragile self-image with this positive affirmation, "I'm good enough, I'm smart enough and doggone it, people like me." But even Stuart had to admit, "Well, not everybody." We all struggle with thinking we're not good enough, smart enough or that people don't like us. As Malcolm Forbes put it, "Too many people overvalue what they are not and undervalue what they are."

In an interview with *Parade Magazine*, *Saturday Night Live* alumnus Dana Carvey, openly admitted feelings of inadequacy: "I feel tremendously guilty about success. Why me? I always feel like I'm six months from oblivion. I know performers who, instead of risking the spotlight and failure, will make sure they screw up before they ever get that far. Either by showing up late for an audition or not writing the piece. I completely understand it. I fight it all the time. That side of me wants to fail because of fear of success. It's easier to hide in failure."

It's interesting isn't it? The people who seem to have it all, by our cultural standards, don't feel like they measure up. Insecurity, it seems, is an equal opportunity malady.

I struggled with all of these esteem issues when I quit my job, moved into that run-down old farmhouse and started my own business. What was worse than going broke in my mind was what other people would think and say if I did. I wanted to be good enough, smart enough and doggone it, I wanted people to like me. It was through this struggle that I reached the conclusion that success was impossible to measure in terms of achievement, competence and recognition because the standard of measurement was arbitrary.

Who was to say I was successful? How much money did I have to make? How much did I have to know? How famous did I have to become? Those are all rat race milestones found on the road *most* traveled. But since I was still subject to the manipulation of reward and punishment I was subconsciously measuring my success by those milestones.

A Diamond in the Rough

He was right. They were there. You couldn't see them with the naked eye but magnified ten times you could see them — tiny flaws. I was examining a diamond under a loop — the small magnifying glass that jewelers use to examine gems. Looking at the ring from the counter, you would never know the diamonds were anything but perfect.

The jeweler explained how the Gemological Institute of America grades diamonds. In addition to a scale for color and finish, diamonds are examined for inclusions (internal characteristics) and blemishes (external characteristics). This is what determines whether a diamond of approximately the same size is worth as little as $1,000 or as much as $5,000. Only an expert examining the diamond under magnification can determine the difference.

As I viewed the diamond under the loop I could see the inclusions. They were small black flecks that looked like tiny chunks of coal from which the diamond originally evolved. I learned that the reason diamonds come in different sizes and shapes — and contain inclusions and blemishes — is because the cutter wants to preserve as much of the precious stone as possible. There would be no diamond left if the cutter attempted to cut the *perfect* stone.

In a sense, we view ourselves like a jeweler examining a diamond under a loop. Every flaw is magnified in our own eyes. We look in the mirror and see physical flaws (blemishes). We look inside ourselves and see behavioral flaws (inclusions). As a result we all too often under-appraise our value. Like diamonds we are unique in size, shape, color and finish. Instead of focusing on our flaws we need to understand the cutter wanted to preserve as much of our worth as possible without completely destroying the stone.

How do you see yourself? How would you describe yourself to other people? Would you describe yourself in positive terms or negative terms? Do you think you could be objective about yourself? Would you err on the side of humility or do you think you might tend to be a little vain?

As I'm asking these questions, you're probably experiencing an internal struggle. On one hand, you don't want to brag on yourself. On the other, you feel like if you don't describe yourself in positive terms you may fall victim to a self-fulfilling prophecy. If I describe myself in negative terms, then I might just live *down* to my expectations. Yet if I describe myself in positive terms people might think I'm egotistical.

If you're a parent, how do you describe your children to other people? Do you describe them in positive or negative terms? Are you objective about your child's abilities? Do you err on the side of humility or do you tend to brag a little bit? I'm betting that you tend to describe your child in positive terms. It's not that you don't know your children's shortcomings. You have to live with them every day. But you see the tremendous potential your children possess. And you tend to view them in terms of what they *can be* rather in terms of what they *aren't*. So it's normal for parents to brag a little bit when it comes to their kids.

Now, how do you think God would describe you? Would he point out your flaws or do you suppose he would describe you in terms of how he created you exactly to the precise specifications required to fulfill your purpose?

Seeing Yourself Intrinsically

Having personally witnessed the inhumanity accompanying Hitler's rise to power in pre-war Germany, Dr. Robert S. Hartman envisioned a science which could organize *good* as effectively as the Nazis organized *evil*. After years of research, Hartman created a new mathematical system called Axiology which successfully orders the values of our everyday experiences. Derived from two Greek words — *xios* (worth or value) and *logos* (logic or theory) — Axiology examines "how we think" and helps us to understand the patterns we use to make judgments.

Hartman identified three distinct dimensions of how we judge and value things:

- **Systemic** - The dimension of formal concepts, ideals, goals, structured thinking, policies, procedures, rules, laws, "oughts" and "shoulds." It is one of perfection.

- **Extrinsic** - This is the dimension of comparisons, relative and practical thinking. It includes the elements of the real, material world, comparisons of good/better/best, and seeing things as they compare with other things in their class.

- **Intrinsic** - The dimension of uniqueness and singularity. It includes people, love, feelings, etc.

Everyone has different strengths and weaknesses in their ability to apply these three dimensions when making decisions. No one uses each dimension equally to make a decision.

From a **systemic** point of view, we measure people against a standard. It can be a system of policies, procedures, rules, laws or a religion. This is a black or white comparison. It's either pass or fail.

When we examine people **extrinsically**, we see them comparatively. They are better than, worse than or about the same as someone else, relatively speaking.

If we view people **intrinsically** we value them for their uniqueness, their essence, their spiritual being. They are the *one* and *only*.

We not only view others but ourselves through the prism of these same three dimensions. If we see ourselves purely through systemic eyes, we'll be frustrated failures. No one can live up to all the rules of any system — even if we get to make the rules.

From an extrinsic viewpoint, we either think more highly of ourselves than we ought or find ourselves lacking.

It is only when you look into the eyes of your soul and view yourself intrinsically that you understand your true value. When viewed from an intrinsic point of view you see yourself exactly as your Creator sees you. You are the one and only. Just as no two snowflakes are alike, you are singularly unique.

Dr. Hartman devoted his life to answering the question, "What is good?" The conclusion he reached was, "A thing is good when it fulfills its definition." Good can be defined as "certain to elicit a specific result" and "something conforming to the moral order of the universe."

Your purpose is God's definition of you. You were created to elicit a specific result. When you are fulfilling your purpose you are conforming to the moral order of the universe.

That is good.

Thinking Supernaturally

When a young shepherd named David learns Israel is being threatened by Goliath he can't understand why the battle-hardened soldiers of the Israeli army are wringing their hands and quaking in their boots. He reasoned that Goliath was a predator just like those he'd encountered as a herdsman. Here's my paraphrase of his assessment of the situation: "When a lion attacked my flock, I killed it. When a bear attacked my flock, I killed it. I don't see any reason why I can't handle a giant." Why was David so calm and confident?

God described David as "a man after my own heart." The heart, in this context, would be defined as the seat of the intellect, will and emotions. This was a nearly universally held view in David's time. Ancient Egyptians thought so little of the brain that they removed it before mummification. It was the *heart* they wanted to preserve.

Since David was a man after God's own heart, he would have possessed the intellect, will and emotions of God. He would have thought like God thought, acted like God would act and felt like God felt. It never occurred to David that he couldn't defeat Goliath. Why? He thought like God. Would God be worried about a lion, a bear, or a giant? Of course not, and neither would someone who possessed the same intellect, will and emotions. David's superhuman knew it could rely on the supernatural abilities it possessed to do whatever his purpose required him to do.

Your animal thinks in tangible terms. It has to see it to believe it. If you can't experience something with your five senses your animal doesn't think it exists. On the other hand, your superhuman has the ability to see the intangible. Think of the tangible (natural) and intangible (supernatural) as two different planes that coexist. They are both real. Your animal only sees the tangible plane because that's all its senses are designed to detect. Your superhuman, however, has the ability to see both planes. Since your superhuman is an extension of God, it thinks like God.

Since your superhuman thinks like God, it assumes it can do whatever is necessary to fulfill your purpose. Your superhuman sees supernatural solutions to natural problems. Your animal's vision is limited to what you and I call reality.

If the Egyptians would have known how powerful the brain was they would have treated it with a little more respect. That computer sitting on top of your shoulders contains more than 100 billion brain cells that are connected and interconnected with 20,000 other cells. According to brain expert Tony Buzan, your brain is capable of generating more thought combinations than there are atoms in the universe.

Let me give you some examples of what these billions of interconnected cells are capable of doing.

Johnny Carson may be the guy who defined late night television for a couple of decades but it all started with the original host of the *Tonight Show*, Steve Allen. I caught the 40th anniversary *Tonight Show* which featured Steve Allen as a special guest. It included several clips from his old programs.

One of the clips featured a segment that he regularly performed called the Answer Man. In this routine he fielded answers from the announcer and then quickly created the question for the answer. One answer he received was, "Vanguard I and Jupiter II." These were names for satellites launched in the 1950s. Steve Allen's answer? "What was the score in the Vanguard — Jupiter game?" That is pure comic genius. What makes his performances even more amazing is that all of the shows were broadcast live back then. There was no editing as there is today.

Steve Allen was also an accomplished musician. Prior to the anniversary show he had composed 4,999 songs. As a demonstration of his creativity he composed song number five thousand on the air using an unorthodox process. As he sat at the piano, he asked *Tonight's* current host Jay Leno to pick three different numbers between one and eight (there are eight notes in an octave on the keyboard). He then pecked out those three notes that corresponded with the numbers of those keys in the octave. He then added the chords and out came the melody of his 5,000th song.

Steve Allen also wrote forty-two books. How was he able to accomplish so much? Steve Allen simply tapped into the unlimited thought combinations that all of us possess but so few of us use. "The great successful men in the world have used their imagination," said Robert Collier. "They think ahead and create their mental picture, and then go to work materializing that picture in all its details, filling in here, adding a little there, altering this a bit and that a bit, but steadily building — steadily building."

It's been said that a true intellectual is someone who can hear *The William Tell Overture* and *not* think of the Lone Ranger. Well, I'm no intellectual because every time I hear *The William Tell Overture* I want to yell "Hi-O Silver, away!" As a youngster, I tuned in with millions of other kids to watch the adventures of the masked man and his faithful companion, Tonto. The Lone Ranger, Tonto and William Tell will always be a trio as far as I'm concerned.

This phenomenon is what psychologists describe as synesthesia. That's where something experienced in one of our senses, such as sight, activates another of our senses, such as sound. Thus the image of an object may conjure up a sound or vice-versa.

A study conducted with a group of ten-year old elementary students reveals how powerful these synesthetic connections can be. First, they gave all the students a large, blank piece of paper and asked them to draw a picture of anything they wanted to. The children drew happy, bright pictures of people laughing, playing and having fun, rainbows, flowers and so on.

Next, the researchers took half of the students and had them listen to happy, cheery, upbeat music for a short time. Again, these children were given a blank sheet of paper and were instructed to draw a picture of anything they chose. Just as before, the pictures were bright and cheery with bold colors. There were a lot of yellows, blues, greens, oranges and reds.

The other half of the class listened to *The Phantom of the Opera* — deep, low, morbid, depressing notes. They too, received a blank sheet of paper and were instructed to draw anything they wished. These children drew dark, scary pictures using a lot of browns, reds and blacks. Their pictures had skulls, blood and destruction. Some of them were just dark whirlwinds of chaos. A few children drew pictures of the bombing of the federal building in Oklahoma City. These sights and sounds were imbedded somewhere deep in the schemas of these children. For whatever reason, they were linked. The sounds activated the images.

Everything we learn is translated into pictures, which are stored in our schemas' archives. We have the unique ability to see things in our mind just as with our eyes. A single stimulus can activate our mental VCR and replay the image.

The Strangest Secret

Comedian Flip Wilson was at his absolute best when he put on a wig, miniskirt and go-go boots to play the part of Geraldine Jones. Geraldine's most famous line was delivered with this flirtatious boast, "What you see is what you get!" And Geraldine was right in a way she, or he if you prefer, never intended. We naturally gravitate to what we see — and what we see is what we get.

This is what Earl Nightingale described in *The Strangest Secret*, a recording he made in 1956 that sold over a million copies. Earl Nightingale had a gold record on his first try and he didn't play an instrument or sing a note. What he did was give birth to the billion dollar audio personal-development industry. Nightingale said the only thing that all of the wise men, teachers, philosophers and prophets have completely and unanimously agreed upon is this — we become what we think about. That's the strangest secret. Think of how powerful this is when you consider that *your* superhuman possesses the intellect, will and emotions of God.

Tuning in to the Right Frequency

During my purposeful transformation, I started experiencing this supernatural thought process. Most of my communication with God in my pre-purpose life was one-way. I'd deliver a monologue commonly referred to as prayer. After all, this is what we're conditioned to do and not getting any audible feedback makes for periods of long silence.

Sometime after discovering my purpose, I decided to take a different approach. I started writing letters to God. First in long hand and then, as I became less technologically-challenged, I started typing these letters on my computer. I did this with the intent that I would be more focused and my mind might not wander as much. But I discovered that my mind still wandered. In fact, it seemed the more I tried to focus and concentrate, the more I was distracted by a barrage of seemingly unrelated random thoughts.

One day as I was dutifully typing away on my letter to God I thought about a phone call I needed to make. I picked up the phone, dialed the number, and only afterwards realized I'd just stopped mid-sentence in my monologue to make the call. Dang it, I'd done it again. I just couldn't stay focused. Then a funny thought popped into my head — could my wandering thoughts, in reality, be God talking to me? Was the reason I wasn't getting any response because I never let him get a word in edgewise? I mean, after all, I *was* asking for guidance. Could his response be that I was supposed to make that phone call right then?

My animal ears were tuned into the frequency of the natural channel. My superhuman was tuned into the frequency of the supernatural channel. In my effort to make sure I was spending *enough* time with God, I failed to understand there is no possible way to spend any *more* time with him. My superhuman is the part of me that *is* God. I'm connected 24/7 as they say — twenty-four hours a day, seven days a week.

This transformed my understanding of God. He wasn't on the outside looking in, *he was on the inside looking out*. I possess the intellect, the will and emotions of God because he resides inside of me. In *Bruce Almighty*, God expresses his frustration with our failure to understand this concept.

> God: *People want me to do everything for them but what they don't under*
> *stand is they have the power. You want to see a miracle, son? Be the miracle.*
>
> Bruce: *Wait, are you leaving?*
>
> God: *Yeah, I see that you can handle things now.*
>
> Bruce: *But what if I need you? What if I have questions?*
>
> God: *That's your problem, Bruce. That's everybody's problem. You keep looking up.*

Being on purpose is being tuned into the supernatural frequency. You don't have to look up to find God — you just look in. He's the superhuman in you.

As I evolve in my purpose that supernatural station comes in clearer with less static from external stimuli. I don't feel guilty anymore when I'm in mid-sentence with God and I think about someone to call or something to do. I now realize that *is* God. I now understand that this is a *dynamic* process of communication — it's a constant dialogue that never ceases.

Imagine, thinking like God — or more accurately, him thinking *through* you. It's the Force. The Force is with you. It's in you. How do mere mortals conceive of putting people on the moon? And even more mind-boggling, how do we actually pull it off? In the words of Peter Nivio Zarlenga, "I am thought. I can see what the eyes cannot see. I can hear what the ears cannot hear. I can feel what the heart cannot feel." Your natural vision allows you to view the tangible. Your supernatural vision allows you to see the intangible. This is the source of our inspiration.

Alan Jackson recorded a moving anthem about the terrorist attacks on 9/11 entitled *Where Were You When the World Stopped Turning.* Jackson will always be credited as the author of the song's lyrics but he's not bashful about revealing the source of his inspiration, "God wrote it. I just held the pencil."

Dream On

This constant stream of supernatural thought continues even in our sleep. Dreams are simply a form of thought taking place in our subconscious when we are not conscious. It might be more accurately described as our *superconscious*. The superconscious solves complex problems and is the source of tremendous creativity.

Should you ever venture to the small town of Hominy, Oklahoma, you're going to discover someone really did "paint the town." That someone is Cha´ Tullis, an artist who brings his Native American heritage to life through murals painted on the walls of buildings throughout the community.

I asked Cha´ where he got the inspiration for his creations. He told me it comes to him in visions at night while he sleeps. He keeps a pad and pencil by his bedside and when awakened from his dreams he sketches what he sees in these *visions*. Each of his murals was first a vision in a dream.

In their book, *The Einstein Factor*, authors Win Winger and Richard Poe tell how inspiration can even be found in a nightmare:

> *Inventor Elias Howe labored long and hard to create the first sewing machine. Nothing worked. Then, one night, Howe had a nightmare. He was running from a band of cannibals — they were so close, he could see their spear tips. Despite his terror, Howe noticed that each spear tip had a hole bored near its tip like the eye of a sewing needle.*
>
> *When he awoke, Howe realized what his nightmare was trying to say: On his sewing machine, he needed to move the eyehole of the needle from the middle down to the tip. That was his breakthrough, and the sewing machine was born.*

"Imagination sets the goal picture which our automatic mechanism works on," said Dr. Maxwell Maltz. "We act, or fail to act, not because of will, as is so commonly believed, but because of imagination." Dr. Maltz, author of the best-selling book *Psycho-Cybernetics,* was a psychiatrist who developed the basis of his self-image psychology from his experiences as a plastic surgeon. He was amazed by the dramatic changes in a patient's self-image as the result of correcting a facial defect: "My scalpel seemed to have magical powers, capable of not only improving the patient's appearance, but of transforming his whole outlook on life."

It was his *failures*, however, that taught him the *self-image* is more powerful than the *physical image*. These failures were not a result of an unsuccessful surgery. It was the failure of many of his patients to see *any* difference *after* the surgery.

How we see ourselves is more powerful than our physiological features. If we can see ourselves *intrinsically*, then we see ourselves as the singularly unique, supernatural, spiritual beings that we are. And we can understand that these mortal animal bodies we're housed in are intricately designed machines to be used in the fulfillment of our assignment on planet earth.

When you know God's purpose for your life you start seeing yourself the way he sees you. The way you are equipped makes sense when you see how he designed you to fulfill your assignment. When you understand your purpose is really God's purpose for you, you start seeing yourself as an extension of him. God speaks to us and operates through us. And that is powerful stuff.

What's Your Reality?

In the movie, *The Truman Show*, Truman Burbank has been the unwitting star of a 24 hour-a-day, 7 day-a-week TV show even *before* his birth. Everyone knows they are members of the cast except Truman. The set is a giant self-contained dome. Truman has a beautiful, loving wife and leads a happy-go-lucky life. It's a perfect life — *too* perfect.

As a young boy, Truman's father drowns while they are sailing. The incident leaves Truman with a fear of the water which prevents him from exploring beyond the boundary of the sea which surrounds the utopian island city where he lives. Of course, his father didn't really die. It was part of the script. The whole episode was an elaborately designed exercise in classical conditioning to keep Truman confined to the island.

A series of events leads Truman to become suspicious that everything isn't quite as it appears. You'd think he would have figured it out years ago. Everything is orchestrated in his life. Every day is eerily like the day before. Everyone, even his wife, mother and best friend, are actors and their every word and action is scripted. Truman is the only actor who is spontaneous because he doesn't know his verse in this carefully crafted version of life's powerful play. He merely responds to the scripted stimuli designed to manipulate him for the pleasure of the viewing audience.

A rare interview with Cristof, the creator and director of *The Truman Show*, provides us with an answer to the obvious question, "Why do you suppose Truman has never come close to discovering the true nature of his world until now?" Cristof turns philosophical: "We accept the reality of the world with which we are presented — it's as simple as that. He could leave at anytime if his was more than a vague ambition. If he was absolutely determined to discover the truth, there is no way we could prevent him." When a former cast member calls in to chastise Cristof for keeping Truman captive he is unrepentant, "I think what distresses you really, caller, is that ultimately Truman *prefers* his cell, as you call it."

Truman does indeed start seeking the truth. First, he escapes the island by facing his greatest fear — he sets out in a sailboat. When Cristof discovers Truman is escaping, he has the stage crew create a storm. That doesn't deter Truman. As a last resort Cristof orders a tidal wave to capsize Truman's boat. Truman survives and eventually his craft collides with the world of his reality — the wall of the dome which serves as the set for his program.

In the end, Truman discovers the truth, and faces it. Cristof, in a last-ditch effort to keep Truman from leaving speaks directly to him, "You're afraid. That's why you can't leave." But Truman is no longer controlled by his fears and takes the leap of faith. He leaves the security of his orchestrated world to venture out into the real world. He seeks the truth, finds it, chooses it and lives it.

I was in a restaurant on Fisherman's Wharf overlooking San Francisco Bay. A radiant sunset framed a silhouette of the Golden Gate Bridge to my left and to my right I could see Alcatraz, the former island prison which once housed such infamous criminals as Al Capone and Machine Gun Kelly. How ironic. Here were two famous landmarks that symbolized both freedom and captivity. The Golden Gate Strait through which so many freedom-seeking immigrants had passed, leads into the Bay which surrounds the island of Alcatraz. An island of captivity in an ocean full of freedom.

Earlier that day I had conducted a seminar and had an interesting conversation with one of the participants. Dan, a postmaster in the Napa Valley, shared a story with me about Ron, a former employee. Ron was a competent letter carrier, Dan explained, but he was also a royal pain in the gluteus maximus. He made life miserable for Dan, his coworkers and everyone else he came in contact with.

One day Dan invited Ron into his office and asked him if he liked his job. Ron said he hated his job. Obviously, it wasn't a good fit. Dan asked Ron how long he'd worked for the Post Office. "Fifteen years." Dan asked him how much longer he planned on working for the Post Office. "Fifteen years." This would give Ron his 30 years and he could retire.

Dan then asked Ron a question that really made him sit up and pay attention, "Do you really want to be as miserable as you are now for the next fifteen years of your life?" Ron said he didn't have a choice — he had bills to pay. "Ron," Dan said, "we *all* have a choice." He then gave Ron ten days of paid leave to think about what he'd do if he weren't a letter carrier. He could check out other careers or just go fishing if he liked.

Ron came back to work and nothing was ever said about what he did during those ten days. Several weeks later he walked into Dan's office and handed him his letter of resignation. Dan nearly fell out of his chair. The employees had a big send-off party for Ron. They made a banner that read: "Ron, glad to see you go!"

About a year later Dan ran into Ron on the street. He said Ron had a big smile on his face and they had a good visit. Ron was now selling real estate and was not only successful but happy.

Ron had been living in a self-imposed Alcatraz for 15 years of his life. In a sense, Dan pardoned Ron from his prison. Ron could have pardoned himself long ago but he thought he had no choice. He had merely accepted the reality of the world with which he was presented.

Like Ron and Truman, many of us live on an island of captivity surrounded by an ocean of freedom. It may not be a prison constructed of concrete and steel, but as Richard Lovelace so eloquently stated, "Stone walls do not a prison make, nor iron bars a cage."

One of our first institute participants, Rita, was the wife of a prison inmate. Through her efforts we had the opportunity to conduct a workshop in the facility where her husband, Gerald, was serving his sentence. Gerald not only discovered his purpose but in a letter to me revealed how he fulfilled it, even while incarcerated:

My purpose is to "help people make sense of the difficult issues in life." I do that by counseling them with encouragement, instruction and correction.

I became aware of this purpose through the responses of many who were facing trying times in their lives. I either noticed or they would ask for help. They have said things like:

- "I was headed straight for trouble. Thank you for warning me."

- "You are such an encourager. I see things more clearly now."

- "You helped me to define the problem and its causes. There really is a solution."

Counseling and teaching is where I'm most comfortable. It has given my life meaning, focus and simplified what I used to struggle with. My purpose has freed me to be myself. No reward or punishment is great enough to cause me to miss my purpose in life.

Gerald's mortal body may have been confined to the boundaries of prison walls but there were no bars strong enough to stop his superhuman from fulfilling his purpose. While in prison he, along with his wife, founded a nonprofit organization that ministers to inmates and their families. Gerald has since been paroled and he continues to fulfill his purpose. The only thing that has changed is he is now helping people make sense of the difficult issues of life on the *outside* as well as with those who are incarcerated.

Perception may not be the ultimate truth, but it is the ultimate reality. We tend to accept the reality of the world with which we are presented. We really don't know what we are capable of if we limit ourselves to that world. "Twenty years from now you will be more disappointed by the things you didn't do than by the ones you did," said Mark Twain. "So throw off the bow lines. Sail away from safe harbor."

To venture beyond the boundaries of our own reality requires us to face our fears. There are storms along the way. But we discover there is more to life than the reality of the world with which we are presented.

If we seek the truth, we will find it. If we choose the truth, it will set us free — free to live beyond the reality of the world with which we are presented.

When Jim Stovall was 17, he was diagnosed with juvenile mascular degeneration which caused his eyesight to gradually go downhill until one day, at the age of 29, he awakened totally blind.

After totally losing his sight, Stovall was listening to an old movie and realized he couldn't follow the action by only hearing the dialogue. So he came up with an idea — why not produce videos for the blind?

Stovall started a company that added a narrative track to an existing piece of film that described the action when the actor's dialogue didn't or couldn't. This enabled the blind to hear a description of the action we see. The concept grew into the Narrative Television Network which now includes over 1,000 cable systems and broadcast facilities. NTN reaches more than 25 million homes in the United States and 11 other countries.

When Stovall lost his sight, the reality of his world changed forever. He says it was the best thing that ever happened to him. As a result of his blindness, he helped change the realities of the world with which millions of sight-impaired people were presented.

"Life has been given to us; we must use it," Stovall writes in his book, *You Don't Have to be Blind to See.* "To reach its full potential, we see the future by taking the next step."

The next step can best be described as the leap of faith.

Your Reality

From an Axiological standpoint, do you tend to value yourself and others intrinsically (singular and unique), extrinsically (compared to others) or systemically (compared to rules)? Record your answers to the following questions. Again, in as much detail as possible:

Do you ever measure yourself compared to a set of cultural, religious, societal, educational, scientific, philosophical standards?

_____

_____

What is the standard or standards and how do you think you measure up?

_____

_____

Do you ever measure yourself compared to other people?

_____

_____

Who do you measure yourself against and why?

_____

_____

How do you measure up?

_____

_____

Do you ever measure yourself against yourself?

_____

_____

What is your standard of measurement?

_____

_____

How do you measure up?

_____

_____

Your Reality: Continued

What have you experienced in your life (childhood, family, culture, religion, education, career, etc.) that has contributed to how you view yourself?

_____

_____

_____

_____

_____

_____

_____

_____

_____

_____

_____

Viewing yourself intrinsically (the way God views you), how would you describe your singular uniqueness? In other words, how would God describe you in terms of the singularly unique purpose for which he created you?

_____

_____

_____

_____

_____

_____

_____

Chapter 7

The Leap of Faith

According to self-development expert Brian Tracy, the reason most people give for wanting to become millionaires is so they won't have to work. I have to agree because I've been there and done that. Prior to the discovery of my purpose, I wanted to get rich so I wouldn't have to work. I was always looking for ways to make lots of money. Most of my attempts resulted in dismal failures that ended up costing me money instead.

One of those schemes was prospecting for gold — that's right, prospecting for gold. A couple of friends of mine were amateur prospectors. They would go up into the Rockies and pan for gold just like those old prospectors of yesteryear. They met another prospector who told them he had been dredging gold from creek beds in the interior of Panama. He came home with a profit of about $60,000 for just a few weeks investment in labor. During his adventures in prospecting he met an old Panamanian man named Enrique who told him about a large vein of gold he had found.

My buddies were intrigued by his story and agreed to accompany their newfound friend to Panama on a prospecting expedition. They wanted to know if I was interested in joining the party. Why not? Maybe we'd hit the mother lode.

Once in Panama, Enrique guided us deep into the interior. As we hiked up into the foothills, we found natives digging in the sides of creek banks panning for gold. They eagerly showed us the fruits of their labors — little bags filled with gold dust. We learned they sold their gold to pawn shops in Panama City. These were poor squatters who lived in shacks. Their primitive mining operations provided them with their primary source of income. And they were doing this with just a pick, a shovel and a pan. I thought about what *we* could do with some serious machinery.

Enrique led us further up the mountainside to the entrance of a crudely dug shaft in the side of the mountain. We picked up several rocks that appeared to have streaks of gold in them and brought them back to the U.S. with us for examination by a geologist. He confirmed that it was gold and came from what appeared to be a very rich vein. You can imagine the visions of wealth that danced in our heads.

We were going to be rich! I'd be a millionaire and wouldn't have to work anymore.

But all was not well in paradise. We learned that we would have to get a mining "concession" — the equivalent of a mineral lease in the United States. That meant dealing with the Panamanian government and the head of the government was Manuel Noriega, the notorious dictator. Graft and corruption were trademarks of his administration and it seemed that bribery was the accepted method for obtaining a concession. That's where we drew the line.

So, Manual Noriega got the gold mine and we got the shaft.

I've often thought about the riches buried in the side of that mountain just waiting to be excavated. But gold has no value as long as it's in the ground. It is only *potential* wealth until it is mined and refined.

Redefining Success

Talk show host Rush Limbaugh often begins his radio program by proclaiming to have "talent on loan from God." While some may consider this blasphemous I consider it to be an accurate acknowledgement of the source of his talent. We all have talent on loan from God. If all of us recognized this fact we would treat our talent as a loan. The money has been transferred to our account, waiting for us to withdraw it, use it and watch it multiply. It is given to us to use or lose. When used, it earns a phenomenal return on investment.

"Wealth, notoriety, place and power are no measure of success whatever," wrote the famous British author, H.G. Wells. "The only true measure of success is the ratio between what we might have been and what we might have done on the one hand and the thing we made and the thing we made ourselves on the other." The true measure of success is determined by what we do with the potential we are entrusted with to fulfill our purpose. We are the stewards of this priceless asset called potential.

In the *Six Million Dollar Man,* Lee Majors starred as a pilot who was rebuilt with a bionic body after a plane crash had left him a part or two short. His bionic makeover cost $6 million. But that was a fictional television program. The actual value of the chemical elements — oxygen, carbon, hydrogen, nitrogen, calcium, phosphorus, and trace amounts of 60 others — in the human body is only about $25 according to the American Chemical Society. However, those elements work together to produce complex biochemicals like hormones, proteins, and nucleic acids worth almost *$6 million.* So, Lee Majors had nothing on you — you're worth six million dollars, too.

Unused talent is as worthless as gold in the ground. God didn't give you a gold mine to let it sit idle. He gave it to you to fulfill your purpose. A chemical reaction is necessary to refine gold. Think back to your high school chemistry class and you'll remember that a catalyst is a substance that initiates a chemical reaction. So what is the catalyst that is required to convert your $25 potential into $6 million worth of supernatural power?

Action!

It is not enough to discover the path of purpose for your life, you have to walk that path to experience the supernatural power that accompanies it.

The Path of God

Put gold and action in the same sentence and Indiana Jones can't be far behind. In *Indiana Jones and the Last Crusade*, Indy must pass a series of three tests to claim the most elusive of all prizes, the Holy Grail. Failure to pass any of the three will result in his death. As if this isn't enough pressure, his father will die if he fails in his quest. The last test is appropriately called *The Path of God.* He must cross a seemingly bottomless chasm to get to a cave on the other side that presumably houses the Grail.

His father's journal reveals what he must do in order to pass this final test: "Only by a leap from the lion's head will he prove his worth." Indy desperately looks for a way to cross the chasm. He can't jump across, it's too far. "It's impossible," he mutters under his breath as he anguishes over what to do. "It's a leap of faith."

Finally, he can wait no longer. Taking a deep breath, he closes his eyes, steps off the edge of the cliff and falls — but only about eighteen inches. His fall is abruptly interrupted by something he can't even *see*. It's a bridge chiseled from stone that is ingeniously camouflaged to blend in with the rock face of the cliff on the other side of the chasm. He safely crosses to the other side on a bridge that only *appeared* when he took *the leap of faith.*

Our purpose guides us on the path of God for our lives. There are times when following that path seems impossible. We can't see how to get there from here. We need a bridge but we can't find it. But the bridge is there — it's simply camouflaged into the scenery of our natural habit. It's only when we take action — the leap of faith — that the bridge for our path is revealed.

It is when we step out in faith — acting on our purpose when we can't see the outcome — that everything comes together at exactly the right time for a supernatural chemical reaction. But without a catalyst there is no chemical reaction. *Action is the catalyst of faith.* No action — no faith. No faith — no results. Faith without *action* is dead.

Anybody can follow a path that is all mapped out, with the outcome guaranteed. That's only natural and the results are natural. Faith requires us to take action on something we can't see. That's supernatural and the results are supernatural. We have been conditioned to seek security, to not take risks, to live lives of quiet desperation. After all, it's better to be safe than sorry.

Your animal tells you, "All you can hope for out of life is a full belly and a roof over your head." But your superhuman is screaming, "Go for it! Take the leap of faith! I know this road! I can see it with my super vision." The test for you on the path of God requires *you* to take the leap. Will you say yes to your purpose? Will you answer destiny's call? Your responsibility is to take action. It is the catalyst for the supernatural.

You are only required to act on your purpose — it's God's job to deliver the results. You act — he delivers. You step out in faith and the bridge on the path of God appears. The road less traveled is the path of God for your life — the path of purpose. And taking that road *does* make all the difference.

You Have to Pamper Yourself

The opposite of faith is fear. It's not *natural* to take the leap of faith. Your animal will tell you there's no bridge and that your leap of faith will result in you going splat on the ground.

Several years ago I was faced with a *leap of faith* choice. I enrolled in an instructor certification class for the Outdoor Adventure Challenge Course, more commonly known as a "ropes course." The manual described it as "an exhilarating maze of cables, logs, platforms, ropes, trees, games and activities offering all ages a physical and mental challenge." That was an understatement — it's like an obstacle course on steroids.

There are *low course elements* which are at ground level and *high course elements* which are suspended from trees and telephone poles some 20-40 feet high.

The low elements are pretty easy to handle. Things get really interesting on the high elements of the course. Participants are paired up. While one partner negotiates the obstacles, the other stays on the ground. A rope is connected to a harness that secures the partner while performing the high wire acts. The partner on the ground holds the other end of the rope that is connected through a pulley on a cable above his partner up in the air. There's no way to fall because you are secured in the harness, which is anchored by your partner on the ground. The worst that can happen is you'll slip off and be left dangling for an embarrassing minute or two until your partner either hoists you back up so you can regain your footing or lowers you safely to the ground.

All of the participants in this particular class were college students. At the age of 40 I was the lone exception. Many of these youngsters were ropes course regulars so it was old hat for them. I had never seen a ropes course, let alone navigate one. I was twice as old as these kids and it showed. During a warm-up game on the first day I bruised the muscle on the inside of my right knee, which hobbled me with a noticeable limp for the duration of the class. I had managed to injure myself before I ever set foot on the actual course.

My partner was a twenty-year-old who claimed rock climbing as his favorite hobby. I had no reason to doubt him — he was muscled, athletic and agile. I, on the other hand, was stiff, sore and ready for a hot shower. He seemingly swung through the trees with Tarzanesque ease while I was on the ground securing him in the harness, not that he needed it. He barely broke a sweat and was at no time in danger of losing his balance. He finished his run through the course with what is called a *pamper pole*. I have no idea why it is called a pamper pole — there is nothing about it that you would associate with the word pamper. It's a 40-foot high telephone pole with foot pegs. You have the *opportunity* to climb to the top and "leap" from the pole to a trapeze bar suspended from another pole at eye level about 10 feet away. This particular course had two pamper poles. One with a trapeze bar, the other had two rings — the same kind that gymnasts use.

Now that my junior partner had finished, it was my turn to play Tarzan. I felt woefully under-qualified. As I was strapping on my harness I asked my young friend if he thought I could negotiate the pamper pole with my bruised knee. "No problem," he assured me. "It just takes balance, not strength." He also suggested I try the pamper pole with two rings. The tra-

80

peze bar, he insisted, just wasn't enough of a challenge. This is probably a good place to stop and note that anyone who is 40 years old ought to know better than to ask advice of someone who is so young he must get a note from his parents if he wants to get married.

I strapped on a helmet, cinched up my harness and I started up the pole. I was in good shape until I set foot on the pegs just below the top and I looked down. If you've ever seen Alfred Hitchcock's *Vertigo*, you'll remember that Jimmy Stewart's fear of heights paralyzes him. The same thing happened to me on top of that pamper pole. I locked up tighter than a government office on a federal holiday.

About that time my bruised knee gave out and my leg started shaking uncontrollably. Not to be outdone, my other leg got into the act. I was now doing a full-fledged Elvis impersonation and the pole started vibrating. After what seemed like an eternity passed, I heard a voice crying in the wilderness — actually it was the course instructor yelling at me from below. I managed to tilt my head far enough to look down and discovered that not only was the course instructor standing at the bottom of the pole but so was every kid enrolled in the course.

The word was out — the old guy was stuck on top of the pamper pole.

I couldn't go back down — my pride wouldn't let me. Besides, I couldn't move anyway. The instructor shouted, "Jim, put your foot up on top of the pole!" He wasn't telling me anything I didn't already know. I knew what my foot was supposed to do — I just couldn't convince it to do it.

It's amazing how religious you can get at times like this. I started making all kinds of promises to God if he would only get me down off that pole. When it became evident that God would not be bribed I started repeating to myself, "Put your foot up on top of the pole. Put your foot up on top of the pole. Put your foot up on top of the pole." Finally, my foot responded to my repeated command and I managed to get both feet on top. This just took my Elvis impersonation to new heights.

Now that I had reached the top I knew exactly what Indiana Jones felt like as he stood at the edge of that cliff. Choosing the rings over the trapeze bar was one more piece of bad advice from Tarzan, Jr. I nearly went cross-eyed trying to focus on those two rings giving a whole new meaning to "a double-minded man is unstable in all his ways."

I had talked myself up to the top of the pole but now that I was faced with the leap of faith I was at a loss for words. Then I looked down and saw the kid who talked me into this standing at the bottom of the pole and thought, *"When I get down from here I'm going to thump him."* That inspired me and I jumped. I caught the rings and latched onto them with a white-knuckled death grip. Now I had another problem — I couldn't let go. The instructor patiently talked my fingers into releasing my grip and I was lowered to the ground. The kids broke into applause. I collapsed and lay on the ground for several minutes completely exhausted. That was the only thing that saved the rock climber's life.

Picture This

I learned a lot about fear that day. There was no way I could fall to the ground. I was safely secured in a harness connected to a rope anchored by my partner. At worst, I might drop a foot or two but wouldn't sustain any injury. Yet I had a hard time convincing my animal body of that.

I like what stunt coordinator Gary Hymes had to say about fear in a *Sports Illustrated* interview, "A veteran stuntman once told me that fear is a picture you've drawn in your mind of what the outcome is going to be. It's a perception that you have. If you're afraid of heights, it's because you don't trust yourself to hold on when you're leaning out over the edge of a tall building. Once you understand that, you can change the outcome, manipulate it to serve you."

If you're afraid to take the leap of faith it's because you have a picture in your mind of a negative outcome. The power of gravity is a natural law. It says that you'll drop like a rock if you take the leap. The power of purpose is a supernatural law. It says that if you take the leap, you're secured in a harness. That harness has a rope that is anchored by your partner and when you're on purpose your partner is God.

There is a wonderful line from the Christmas classic, *Miracle on 34th Street*: "Faith is believing in something when common sense tells us not to." There are times when we need *uncommon sense*. Common sense is natural, uncommon sense is supernatural. Your animal possesses common sense. Your superhuman possesses uncommon sense. Both are valuable. Common sense is a good thing. It serves a valuable function in our lives. It keeps us from doing stupid stuff. But there are times when we have to trust our superhuman uncommon sense. That's faith.

Here's something that will help you change the picture of the outcome in your mind. Remember, it's not *your* purpose; it's *God's* purpose for *you*. He didn't give you your purpose to watch you fail. He gave it to you so you can succeed. If you're on purpose then you can't fail. If you fail that means God fails. And God can't fail. The path of purpose is a supernatural journey. It supercedes natural laws. Your superhuman doesn't fear the leap of faith because it knows God is on the other end of the rope. The outcome is in *his* hands. Remember, you're in the efforts business and he's in the results business. Take care of your end of the deal and he'll take care of his.

This doesn't mean you won't experience episodes of failure. Winston Churchill, whose life was peppered with many monumental setbacks, was able to put them in perspective, "The secret of success is to go from failure to failure with enthusiasm." The word enthusiasm means to be *inspired*. Inspire is derived from the Greek word *entheos*. En + theos = in God or God within. Your superhuman is God within you. Your superhuman is inspired by a singular motive — purpose. When you are on purpose you are *possessed* — the power of God possesses you.

"You gain strength, courage and confidence by every experience in which you really stop to look fear in the face," said Eleanor Roosevelt. "You are able to say to yourself, 'I lived through this horror. I can take the next thing that comes along.' You must do the thing you think you cannot do." Before I completed my ropes course certification class I went back and jumped off the pamper pole several more times. Each time it got a little easier.

As I've traveled the path of purpose in my life I have taken many leaps of faith. Each leap gets a little easier. I'm learning to focus more on my efforts and less on the results. I do my job and God does his. I used to see a picture of negative outcomes in my mind. But with purpose as my picture, the outcome is out of my hands. I focus on the destination and let God take care of how to get me there. I'm only required to take action. The outcome is *his* problem, not mine.

I still feel all of the emotions that come when faced with pamper pole situations. But that's OK. It doesn't mean I let those emotions control me. Put in their proper perspective those emotions work for me. Even Tiger Woods, the world's greatest golfer, feels pressure: "I always feel pressure. If you don't feel nervous, that means you don't care about how you play. I care about how I perform. I've always said the day I'm not nervous playing is the day I quit."

Being "nervous" simply means you care. It means you're *up* to the challenge.

What's the Worst That Can Happen?

In the film classic, *The Treasure of Sierra Madre*, Fred C. Dobbs (Humphrey Bogart) and Curtin (Tim Holt) are two down-and-out Americans stuck in Tampico, Mexico during the 1920s. They run into Howard, an old prospector played by Walter Huston. After hearing Howard's gold prospecting tales, the three of them pool their resources and head to the hills to strike it rich.

Along the way, they are attacked by bandits, trek through jungle and desert but finally strike pay dirt. They set up a crude mining operation and after months of toil, they make their fortune. Then the plot gets interesting.

They load bags filled with gold dust on their burros and head back to civilization. Dobbs becomes crazed with greed, and makes off with the whole fortune. Bandits catch up with Dobbs and kill him. Unprocessed gold dust is almost indistinguishable from sand and that's exactly what the bandits believe it is. They break open the bags and a dust storm carries the gold dust back to the hills from which it came.

When Howard and Curtin discover what has happened, you can imagine their shock and disbelief. But then they are struck by the irony of the situation. The gold has been returned to the earth from which it was taken and they are left penniless.

Disbelief is replaced by hysterical laughter. It is at this moment that Tim Holt delivers a classic line, "You know, the worst ain't so bad when it finally happens. Not half as bad as you figure it will be before it happens."

I've been faced with financial ruin on more than a couple of occasions. I was able to get through them by asking myself this question, "What's the worst that can happen?" The answer was, "I'll go broke." Then I asked myself, "Can I accept that?" The answer was, "Been there, done that." When I reconciled myself to the fact that I had been broke before and that I could always make money, the worst didn't seem half as bad as I'd figured.

The *worst* is just a picture of an outcome in our minds.

It's Your Choice

Sondra went to a showing at a local museum featuring the work of several *French Impressionists* including Monet, Renoir, Picasso, and others. As she studied one of Monet's paintings that featured a beautiful blur of pastel colors, she overheard a couple of grade school boys critiquing the great artist's work. A picture may be worth a thousand words but one of the youngsters was able to sum up his assessment of Monet with only four. He looked at the painting, turned to his friend and stated with unabashed confidence, "I could do that!"

Before I switched my major to animal science I was — I know this is hard to believe — an art major. I'm really a pretty good artist. In fact, I would agree with the young art critic that Sondra encountered — when I look at a Monet or a Renoir, I say, "I could do that!" And I'll bet with a little practice (I haven't painted in years) I could paint something that would pass, in the eyes of most people, something that would look like a Monet or Renoir.

As an art student I discovered there were many artists who possessed talent. And I know there are many people who have never so much as doodled on their Big Chief tablet in the first grade that are capable of works of art. I believe the young man assessing Monet's painting may, in reality, be capable of painting just as well as Monet himself.

Many of us stand in life's art gallery and say to ourselves, "I could do that," but never do. We stand and stare at the blank canvas of our lives and think of all the reasons we can't, so we never start.

Saying "I can do it" is only the first step. To succeed our words have to evolve into faith. And in the words of William Newton Clark, "Faith is the daring of the soul to go farther than it can see." We can never succeed if we never start. Action doesn't guarantee success, but without it we are assured of failure.

The reason the paintings of Monet and Renoir are hanging in art galleries is because they took some brushes, dabbed them in some paint and decorated a canvas. If they had not acted in faith on their talent, we would have never known who they were.

Impressionism is defined as "depicting the natural appearances of objects by means of dabs or strokes of primary unmixed colors in order to simulate actual reflected light." I didn't go to the art show with Sondra because I'm just not that impressed with impressionists. I am a realist — in every sense of the word — but even more so when it comes to art. Give me Norman Rockwell, Charles Russell and Frederick Remington.

But we are all really impressionists. Our talents consist of primary unmixed colors. Until we apply them we make no impression. We must dab and stroke until those talents reflect our actual light.

We can go through life looking at other artists' paintings and say, "I could do that!" Or we can borrow a line from Bo Jackson and "just do it." *Our* picture may be worth a thousand words, but if it is never painted those words are never spoken.

In his book, *The Soul's Code; In Search of Character and Calling*, James Hillman describes what he calls the "acorn theory." An acorn in itself reveals nothing of its destiny but it contains the blueprint of an oak tree. It needs only to be planted. Each person, like an acorn, bears a uniqueness that asks to be lived.

You possess the seed of your destiny. But it is up to you to plant it.

The ropes course manual had a section entitled *Challenge by Choice*, which explained: "Each participant voluntarily and freely engages in any activity. The degree and extent of participation remains the individual's own choice, based on what the person can comfortably and willingly risk. No one is ever required, forced, or coerced to do any activity." Challenge by choice reminds me of a scene from *Bruce Almighty*, when God lays out the conditions for Bruce to play God.

> *God: You have all my powers. Use them in any way you choose. There are two rules. You can't tell anybody you're God. Believe me, you don't want that kind of attention. And you can't mess with free will.*
>
> *Bruce: Can I ask why?*
>
> *God: Yes, you can! That's the beauty of it!*

God isn't going to force his purpose upon you. You have to seek it. And once you discover it, you still have to act on it. God will place people and circumstances in your path but you have to choose whether to play or pass. He's given each of us that wonderful yet terrible gift of free will — the power of choice.

"The vision must be followed by the venture," said Vance Havener. "It is not enough to stare up the steps — we must step up the stairs."

And when you get to the top, you'll have the opportunity to take the leap of faith. But it's your choice.

Risk

Look back over your life and think of a time when you took a great risk — a time when you really pushed yourself out of your comfort zone. Maybe it was in a competition, in business, in a social setting, in a relationship, at work or in school. Describe that experience in as much detail as possible.

_____

_____

_____

_____

_____

_____

_____

_____

_____

_____

_____

_____

_____

_____

_____

_____

_____

_____

Risk: Continued

Now record your answers to the following. Again, in as much detail as possible.

How did you feel?

_____

_____

_____

How did it impact you?

_____

_____

_____

How did it impact others?

_____

_____

_____

What needs in Maslow's hierarchy did you have to overcome to take this risk?

_____

_____

_____

What fears did you have to overcome?

_____

_____

_____

If you don't feel like you've ever taken a great risk, write down the reason why you haven't — in other words, what are you fearful of or what need seems to be holding you back?

_____

_____

_____

Chapter 8

It Hurts So Good

Keith worked at a service station in my hometown where Harold, one of the local characters, was a regular customer. Harold was a very well-to-do cattleman, banker and businessman but you'd never guess it from his dress or manner. He always carried a saddle in his pickup which was not unusual because this was cow country. Pickups, cowboys, saddles and horse trailers were part of the local landscape.

But instead of carrying his saddle inside the bed of his pickup Harold always had it slung haphazardly over the side panel on the bed and didn't even bother to tie it down. One day, when he pulled into the station to gas up, curiosity got the best of Keith. "Do you think you might lose your saddle carrying it like that?" he asked. Harold looked at Keith and replied matter-of-factly, "Hell, I've lost four saddles carryin' 'em like that!" Harold kept carrying his saddles on the side of his pickup bed and he kept on losing them.

It's been said that to keep doing the same thing over and over but to expect different results is the definition of insanity. If that's true, then all of us are at least a little crazy.

Psychologists will tell you that people rarely come in for therapy unless they are experiencing some degree of pain. After all, therapy requires an investment of time, money and effort. It's human nature to hope and wish for different results without any investment of time, money or effort on our part. We may know that we need to change, but until the pain is great enough we usually won't do anything about it.

Harold had enough money to keep on buying new saddles when he lost them. The loss of a saddle didn't create enough pain for him to stop carrying it on the side of the pickup. There was not severe enough *adverse* consequences to cause him to evaluate his behavior. He needed a little *more* adversity.

Adversity creates some degree of discomfort. Severe adversity causes pain. But adversity performs a valuable function in our lives. It is a normal part of life. The timeline between birth and death is filled with the peaks and valleys of the human experience. I can tell you that being on purpose doesn't eliminate those peaks and valleys. But being on purpose will help you understand the necessary role adversity plays in our lives.

We naturally avoid pain and suffering. This is part of our *natural* defense mechanism. We naturally strive to survive. We are at the top of the food chain so being hunted and killed to feed another species is of no concern to us. While other animals in the *natural habitat* are just trying to eat and keep from being eaten, we are trying to find meaning in our lives.

This search for meaning is what led psychiatrist Viktor Frankl to develop what he called Logotherapy or *meaning-centered* psychotherapy. "It is one of the basic tenets of Logotherapy that man's main concern is not to gain pleasure or to avoid pain but rather to see a meaning in his life," wrote Frankl. "That is why man is even ready to suffer, on the condition, to be sure, that his suffering has meaning."

Dr. Frankl, who was Jewish, had the opportunity to flee Austria with his wife before the Nazis annexed the country during World War II but it would require him to leave his elderly parents behind. He reasoned that if Logotherapy were valid, he must prove it to himself. He elected to remain in Austria knowing the consequence may subject him and his family to the barbaric cruelty of Hitler's Third Reich.

Eventually Frankl's entire family was incarcerated in concentration camps. He was the sole survivor. Survivors endured suffering the rest of us can only imagine in our worst nightmares. But it was in this incubator of death and human suffering that Frankl validated Logotherapy.

Dr. Frankl chronicled his experiences and conclusions in his book, *Man's Search for Meaning.* Frankl discovered that meaning could be found in the worst of human conditions. "The more one forgets himself," he wrote, "by giving himself to a cause to serve or another person to love — the more human he is and the more he actualizes himself." Frankl observed an interesting phenomenon about the plight of his fellow prisoners. Those who survived all had something in common, they had something of importance yet to complete in their lives.

No Pain, No Gain

"The story of the human race is the story of men and women selling themselves short," said Maslow. In his book, *Maslow on Management,* he states that we must teach "self-development, self-actualization, discipline and hard work in the fullest development of one's own talents or capacities, one's own genius."

> *This is crucially necessary today because so many young people are making a distorted interpretation of the pervasive psychology of growth and self-actualization. More dependent, more indulged, more oral, more passive people are interpreting this philosophy of self-actualization to mean "waiting for inspiration," waiting for something to happen, waiting for something to grab them, waiting for some peak experience which will tell them automatically and without effort what their destiny is and what they should do. Part of this feeling of self-indulgence is that anything which is self-actualizing should be enjoyable.*

Maslow goes on to say that while this is ultimately true in principle, it's not always immediately true.

> *Cultivating one's capacities can be hard work, can be distasteful in itself (even though it may simultaneously be enjoyed by those who understand it as taking*

*a necessary step toward the ultimate goal of self-actualization by a commit-
ment to a particular destiny).*

*This whole philosophy of waiting for things to happen instead of making them
happen, of loafing and loitering during this waiting period instead of regard-
ing talent as requiring teaching, exercise, rehearsal, training, hard work and
the like, has to be counteracted.*

Maslow's observations could be condensed into the creed body builders live by, "No pain,
no gain."

Whenever people tell me they are struggling with finding their purpose, I tell them that's
good. There is value in the struggle. While researching his book, Po Bronson encountered a
young man who was struggling and reassured him, "I think the depth of your struggling is the
sign there's something there. Something in you that's trying to get out. People who don't have
passions don't struggle."

My experience has taught me the search is not only a struggle but the discovery brings
with it a whole new struggle. But it's a good kind of struggle, one where you know there's
value in it, that it's worth it.

Stress for Success

Bronson observes that many people are looking for what he calls "brain candy." But his
research revealed people who have "found their place weren't reporting twenty-four-hour
highs." That concurs with what I've found. Life hasn't gotten easier for me. In fact, it's much
more challenging. But it's never boring.

People today constantly complain about stress. They have stress on the job, in their mar-
riages, with their kids. It is often attributed to work overload. In reality, it is more often the
opposite. It is work *underload*. In their book, *Stressless Selling* by Frances Stern and Ron
Zemke, the authors found people suffering from work underload report the following symptoms:

- The need for a pick-me-up at work (food, caffeinated drinks, cigarettes).
- Their minds wondering during meetings and when working alone.
- Sometimes staring blankly and thinking nothing at all for periods of time.
- Feeling low or flat when at work.
- Dragging themselves out of bed in the morning.
- Job dissatisfaction with no obvious cause.
- Few feelings of pride about tasks accomplished on the job.

If you are suffering from the above symptoms, you aren't maximizing your potential.
Driving around in first gear is boring. Why not kick it into overdrive and see what your $6

million machine can do? But be prepared when you do because you will run head on into adversity.

While you may experience hardship as you accelerate on the road of purpose you'll be better off for the challenge it brings. "The harder the conflict, the more glorious the triumph," said Thomas Paine, who knew a thing or two about adversity. "What we obtain too cheap, we esteem too lightly; it is dearness only that gives everything value. I love the man who can smile in trouble that can gather strength from distress and grow brave by reflection. Tis the business of little minds to shrink; but he whose heart is firm, and whose conscience approves his conduct, will pursue his principles unto death."

Adversity is not bad. It's uncomfortable, inconvenient and sometimes painful, but it's the most powerful catalyst for positive change and growth that we possess. Adversity is exactly what you need to mine and refine the reserves of gold you possess. No pain, no gain. Resistance builds strength. To increase strength, you must push yourself beyond your current capability. To do that, you lift heavier weights or do more repetitions, or both. You exercise that muscle or muscle group to the point of exhaustion or failure. You lift until you can't lift any more.

That "failure" is the catalyst that causes the muscle to repair and grow. By repeating this process over time you are able to lift more weight and do more repetitions. It leaves you a little sore but you get over it. The bottom line is this — failure is a requirement for success. Without pushing yourself to failure or exhaustion, you'll never be able to lift more.

The word fail might best be defined as "to fall short." Once you realize that failure is not the end of the world, you simply try again — and again and again — until you finally succeed. This is an exhausting process. But I like this definition of exhaust I found in the dictionary: "To fully develop." You'll never develop your full potential as a person without experiencing failure and exhaustion.

Scott Adams, creator of the popular comic strip *Dilbert,* puts failure into its proper perspective: "Most success springs from an obstacle or failure. I became a cartoonist largely because I failed in my goal of becoming a successful executive."

Wear Your Scars Proudly

Ray Charles lost his younger brother in a traumatic accident when they were small children. While playing in the backyard, his brother fell headfirst into a tub full of water. Ray wasn't strong enough to pull his brother from the tub and he drowned. Life got even tougher for Ray. Glaucoma robbed him of his eyesight. He was completely blind by the age of seven and was sent to the St. Augustine School for the Blind in Florida.

This was in the days of segregation and the school had a white side and a black side. Now stop and think about that for a minute. A school where blind children are segregated by the color of their skin would have to seem like a cruel joke. Young Ray dreamed of playing the

92

piano and the school had one in its music room but the music room was on the white side of the school. Therefore Ray wasn't allowed to use the music room except during times the white children weren't using it.

If being blind and black in a segregated school wasn't enough, Ray had another cross to bear. His family was so poor that Ray's folks couldn't afford to buy him a bus ticket home during the holidays. But that cross was his salvation. All of the other children returned to their homes during the holidays — leaving the music room all to Ray. And that's when he honed his skills on the piano.

Ray's mother passed away when he was fifteen years old. But, as he wrote in his autobiography, adversity proved to be the catalyst that propelled him, "…the two greatest tragedies in my life — losing my brother and then my mom — were, strangely enough, extraordinarily positive for me. What I've accomplished since then, really, grows out of my coming to terms with those events."

When I was in the second grade, my mother showed up at school one day and spoke to my teacher. The teacher asked me to clean out my desk and I left with my mother. Test results from an earlier visit to the doctor revealed I had Nephritis, a serious kidney disease. After spending two weeks in the hospital, close to death, I recovered but was bedfast for the next six months.

I assumed that I would join my former classmates in the third grade the following school year. Then I learned I would have to take the second grade over. I was devastated. Many of my new classmates the next year assumed I failed the second grade because I wasn't smart enough to pass. And I felt every bit the failure. They teased me and called me stupid. Their cruel remarks were much more painful than the year of illness I had been through. Just thinking about that now still brings back painful memories.

Life seemed so unfair then. But I can look back now and realize that the adversity I faced at such a young age made me tough and prepared me to deal with the even greater adversities I face now. It turned out to be a defining event in my life. I learned to become calloused to the remarks and opinions of other people.

"God will not look you over for medals, degrees or diplomas," wrote Elbert Hubbard, "but for scars." I can tell you where every scar is on my body. And I can tell you the story behind every one of those scars. But scar tissue is tougher than your unblemished skin. The wounds incurred from the taunts of my classmates made me tough and determined. No one is going to say or do anything to me that will deter me from fulfilling my purpose now.

Wear your scars proudly. They are evidence that you have been in the battle — and survived.

Don't Get Too Comfortable

Gail Sheehy learned some interesting things while doing research for her book, *Understanding Men's Passages: Discovering the Map of Men's Lives.* I think her findings can be applied to anyone regardless of gender. For example, she writes about "exit events" in our lives.

Exit events are the things we experience in the second halves of our lives, such as the departure of grown children or the sudden death of friends. These events remind us of our mortality and serve as rites of passage into the final chapters of our lives.

"Traditionally, people have spent their young and middle adulthood working hard so that they can be 'comfortable' in their old age," she writes. "But that's the last thing we want to be — too comfortable. We want to be active, engaged, useful and sometimes tossing in our sleep at night — thinking about how to pursue our passion tomorrow. Men who live to be 100 tend to be their own bosses and do not retire early."

If I win the Readers Digest Sweepstakes tomorrow, I'll keep doing what I'm doing. I like the challenges that come with the fulfillment of my purpose. It's "challenge by choice" and I love it. And on the days when I get beat up — and believe me, there are a bunch of them — I remind myself the reason I'm doing what I'm doing is because I'm on purpose. I can persevere because I'm on purpose. As Robin, one of our Institute graduates so aptly put it, "Your purpose will pull you through any adversity."

Where Do You Find Inspiration?

What do you think of when you think of Dolly Parton? Uh huh, I know — two things come to mind. Dolly is a wonderful entertainer and she is down-home real. Like anyone who has become successful, she faced a lot of adversity. As fellow entertainer Roy Clark said, "Going from a nobody to a somebody is a thousand miles of hard road." In her autobiography, Dolly reveals what kept her going when the going got tough.

> *My high school was small. So during a graduation event, each of us got to stand up and announce our plans for the future. "I'm going to junior college," one boy would say. "I'm getting married and move to Maryville," a girl would follow. When my turn came, I said, "I'm going to Nashville to become a star." The entire place erupted in laughter. I was stunned. Somehow, though, that laughter instilled in me an even greater determination to realize my dream. I might have crumbled under the weight of the hardships that were to come had it not been for the response of the crowd that day. Sometimes it's funny the way we find inspiration.*

Nobody's laughing at Dolly now, but that laughter was the fuel that fed Dolly's fire. Look at the adversities you face in life as trials by fire. The potential that God has given to you to fulfill your purpose has great value but it has to be mined and refined. 22 tons of earth must be removed to uncover one ton of gold ore. It takes one ton of ore to produce one-third of an ounce of gold. Heat is used to refine gold. It burns away all the dross that contains all of the impurities and foreign material. For your potential to be fully realized you have to get rid of all the stuff that covers up its true value. Adversity performs that function. Sometimes it *is* funny the way we find inspiration — it shows up disguised as adversity.

Monty, a good friend and one of my first consulting clients, quit a secure job to start his own irrigation equipment business. It was tough going in the beginning. One day he was having lunch in the local café when he overheard his biggest competitor tell someone that Monty would never make it in the irrigation business.

Monty went on to become the largest center pivot sprinkler dealer in North America. He never forgot what the competitor said about him in the café. It inspired him. Sometimes it's funny the way we find inspiration. The competitor should have kept his mouth shut — it was he who went out of business.

I attended a question and answer session with Tom Peters after one of his presentations. Someone asked him what he considered to be his greatest failure. "When I was fired from McKinsey & Company," was his answer. Peters gained famed as coauthor of *In Search of Excellence* in the early 1980s. The book was a bestseller — but not with the management at McKinsey where Peters was a partner in the consulting group. It seems his book clashed with the management's philosophy.

"Getting fired was the best thing that ever happened to me," Peters told us. Why? His "failure" forced him out of his nest at McKinsey. His greatest failure was the catalyst that propelled him to even greater success. He now has his own company, travels the world speaking and consulting and has gone on to write several more best-sellers.

A boy named Joseph ticked off his brothers when he told them about a dream he had that revealed his purpose in life. They thought selling him into slavery would take him down a notch or two. He found favor with his master but then was framed for a crime he didn't commit and jailed. Because of a "chance" encounter with a fellow prisoner he was given the opportunity to interpret a dream of the Pharaoh of Egypt.

Pharaoh recognized the supernatural power of purpose in Joseph and gave him the keys to his kingdom, the most powerful kingdom on earth at that time. So Joseph was transformed from a slave and convict into the most powerful man in the world. That's the transformational power of purpose. But Joseph would have never been in position to receive the keys to the kingdom had he not been enslaved and imprisoned.

Creators Syndicate represents many of the best writers and artists in syndication to newspapers around the country. Creators came out of nowhere in 1987 to capture some of the biggest hitters in the business. But Richard Newcombe, the founder of Creators, got off to a rocky start.

According to *Investors Business Daily*, his new firm was losing tens of thousands of dollars a week and teetered on the brink of bankruptcy before it even celebrated its first anniversary. On December 26, 1987, Newcombe discovered someone had a merry Christmas at his expense. The company's entire computer system had been stolen on Christmas Day.

This would be enough for a lot of people to question whether the deck had been stacked against them. But not Newcombe. "I had an unshakable faith. I mean I really had it in my head that if I had to, I'd crawl over broken glass. I'd live in a tent — it was going to happen. And I think when you have that kind of steely determination — sort of like Margaret Thatcher or Winston Churchill — people get out of the way."

I like his choice for examples of determined people. Churchill was known for his bulldog-like perseverance and Margaret Thatcher was known as the Iron Lady. Both left big footprints not only in Great Britain but the world.

"Within every adversity lies the seed of an equivalent or greater benefit," wrote Napoleon Hill in his bestselling book, *Think and Grow Rich*. When the Grinch stole Richard Newcombe's Christmas in 1987 it may have been just what he needed to hone his steely determination.

If Joseph hadn't been sold into slavery, he probably would have ended up herding sheep back home. His "thousand miles of hard road" started when God revealed his purpose to him in a dream. Joseph's journey from sheepherder to world leader took years but he was able to persevere because he was on purpose.

Without adversity we would succumb to our animal natures. Like a hog in a mud hole we would lie there fat, dumb and happy — but completely clueless. We wouldn't change and we wouldn't grow. Change and growth are difficult — *even when you are on purpose.*

I used to belong to a health club that conducted abdominal exercise classes three times a week. The instructor was a former neurosurgeon turned fitness guru known to the class as *Dr. Abs*. A more appropriate name would have been the Exercise Nazi. If you outfitted him in a uniform and gave him a riding crop and a monocle he could have passed for a member of the Gestapo. "You *vill* crunch your abdominals and you *vill* like it!"

On Fridays, those who were tough enough — or who lacked good sense — participated in a form of modern torture or as Dr. Abs called it, an extended workout. One Friday I decided I was tough enough. I joined them.

About half-way through the workout I thought I was dying. I had muscles aching in places I didn't know I had muscles. It was at this point the Exercise Nazi barked out to no one in particular, "Pain, suffering and perseverance make for joy!" Then he wryly added, "You ought to be feeling real joyful right now."

Joyful? Dr. Abs must have been an admirer of Charles Spurgeon, the famous 19th century English clergyman who said, "Adversity, however it may appear to be our foe, is our true friend; and, after a little acquaintance with it, we receive it as a precious thing — the prophecy of a coming joy. It should be no ambition of ours to traverse a path without a thorn or stone."

We can look back on our adversities and know the pain was worth the gain. A Portuguese proverb puts it this way, "What was hard to bear is sweet to remember."

Or, as John Cougar Mellencamp expressed in the words of one of his songs, "It hurts so good."

Adversity

During your life you have experienced times of adversity that have served to mine and refine the potential you possess. Look back to a time (or times) when you faced a great adversity — a very difficult time in your life — and describe it in as much detail as possible.

_____

_____

_____

_____

_____

_____

_____

_____

_____

_____

_____

_____

_____

_____

_____

_____

_____

_____

_____

_____

Adversity: Continued

Now, write your answers to the following questions. Again, in as much detail as possible.

How did you feel?

_____

_____

_____

_____

How did you overcome it?

_____

_____

_____

_____

What did you learn about yourself through this experience?

_____

_____

_____

_____

What good can you identify as a result of this experience?

_____

_____

_____

_____

Chapter 9

Doing What Comes *Supernaturally*

"It is important to remember that we cannot become what we need to be by remaining what we are," writes Max DePree in his book, *Leadership is an Art*. But becoming what we need to be requires us to engage in that most challenging of human endeavors — change. New Year's resolutions are made — and broken. All of us have been disappointed with our inability to change certain behaviors.

We're all addicts. We're addicted to our past patterns of behavior. Anyone who has tried to lose weight has experienced the frustration of addiction. We're addicted to our old eating and exercise behaviors. Our animals are conditioned to an eating pattern. That's the whole problem. We are so well trained that we do what we do without realizing we're doing it. And when we do realize what we're doing and we want to change it, we discover that we fall right back into our old patterns of behavior. We truly are creatures of habit. As Aristotle said, "We are what we repeatedly do."

In Dennis Sherwood's book, *Unlock Your Mind*, he notes that most people wear between eight and fourteen items of clothing and it only takes us a few minutes to get dressed. Now here's something that will shock you. If you wear eight items there are theoretically 40,320 different ways to get dressed. If you wear fourteen items that number jumps up to 87,178,291,200.

You probably put your clothes on in the same order every day in the same way. Now, just try *changing* the order of items in the way you get dressed. If you wear eight items of clothing see how many of the 40,320 different ways you can master. You'll probably find that you're addicted to your current pattern.

Like Cows Standing At A New Gate

We're like cows standing at a new gate. You can turn a bunch of cows out into a new pasture and before long they will have walked the perimeter and learned the boundaries established by the fence. Then, let's say you decide to build a new gate somewhere along that perimeter for the purpose of moving the cows to a different pasture. You open the gate, jump on your horse, roundup the cows and start driving them to the gate you've just built. And they'll just walk right through it, right? Wrong. You'll find yourself chasing those cows up and down the fence line for awhile. Why? Their *schema* tells them that there is no gate, only a fence.

Let's revisit our lesson about schemas from chapter two. Schema is the root word of schematic. Think of a schema as a type of schematic diagram in your head. An electrical schematic diagram is a blueprint that shows how something is wired. Your schemas are blueprints that reveal how *you* are wired. These schemas exert a powerful influence on how you process information. Let's take a look at how these schemas are formed.

You never forget how to ride a bike. But do you remember how you *learned*? When you first learn to ride a bike, you have to concentrate on every move — you make mistakes and correct them. After a while you're riding without even thinking about it — it's *natural*. A neural pathway is being formed, or encoded, in your brain each time you consciously go through the steps of learning to ride the bike.

Neuro is the root word of neuron, which Webster describes as "a grayish or reddish granular cell with specialized processes that is the fundamental functional unit of nervous tissue." These neurons create neurological pathways in your brain whenever you perform a task. Each time you repeat a task the same way, you strengthen the pathway, or connections between the neurons. The more repetitions, the stronger the connection. The more you repeat the behavior, the more ingrained the neurological pathways. It creates what might best be described as a rut.

So how do we create new ruts? We have to throw a *road block* in the neurological pathway by breaking the routine. When we break the routine, we stimulate the brain to create a new pathway instead of just strengthening the old one.

We tend to *see* things that fit our pre-existing schemas and are *blind* to things that don't. Our schemas become filters for incoming information with which we do one of three things — accept it, reject it or reshape it to fit what we already believe. This is an unconscious process. That's why it's so hard to change a way of thinking or a habit. The neural pathway is now a rut. We've all heard that practice makes perfect. But that's not necessarily true. Practice makes *permanent*. Research suggests that once a schema is fully developed it is permanent.

This is why change is so difficult. The encouraging news is we can form new schemas. This is best accomplished indirectly and implicitly, as opposed to directly and rationally. Indirect and implicit learning (observing) has more influence on the encoding processes, which trigger behaviors, than explicit and direct learning (telling).

If you want to drive the cows through the new gate, here's how you do it. You push them up close to the gate and then back off a little bit. Before long one of them will start looking and sniffing, inching ever closer to the imaginary wires they see in their schema. Then that cow will cautiously walk through the gate, followed by another then another until the rest hightail it through on a dead run. Some will even jump as they go through trying to hurdle the imaginary gate.

One of the most critical things I've learned as a consultant is this. People — like cows standing at a new gate — have to reach the right conclusions on their own. You can tell them something over and over but until the light bulb goes on in *their* head it doesn't matter. It's only when *they* see the opening that they'll go through the gate.

Then a new schema is born.

It's Easier Done Than Said

While attending a boat and tackle show Sondra and I found a booth featuring an unusual looking fishing pole. It looked like a modern version of an old cane pole. The line ran through the inside of the pole — not on the outside through guides like other poles. The pole telescoped out to twelve feet in length but was only about four feet long when collapsed.

Curiosity got the best of people looking at this unusual pole and they had to ask the obvious question, "How do you use this thing?" That's when the salesman made his pitch. He handed them the pole and told them, "It's easier done than said." I had to laugh — easier done than said? Didn't he have that backwards? Shouldn't it be easier said than done?

How do you really learn a new skill? Someone can explain how to do it but the instructions usually fall far short of what you need to know. Research shows that we retain 10% through reading, 20% through seeing, 30% through hearing, 50% through seeing *and* hearing, 70% through collaboration and 80% by *doing*.

Learning a new behavior really is easier done than said.

What Would Andy Do?

Parenting, for the most part, is learned on the job. Most parents have a pretty good idea of what they don't want to do. You don't want to do the things that really bugged you about your own parents. Then you have kids. And they become teenagers. And you tell them to be home by midnight. Being the dutiful parent you wait up — just out of concern, mind you. Then, when the clock strikes twelve, no teenager. Ten after, no teenager. Half past midnight and still no teenager.

Now before I take the next step, I want to remind you that you made a conscious decision to do things differently than your parents. You grew up watching Andy Griffith deal with Opie in a much kinder, gentler manner than what you experienced at home. So you were going to handle this like Andy.

Then your teenager quietly opened the front door and peered sheepishly into the living room to see if the coast was clear. He didn't have to look far because you met him at the door. Your eyes were bulging and the veins were sticking out on the side of your neck as you stuck your finger in his face and announced in a voice that would make a drill sergeant flinch, "Boy, if you want to live to see your twenty-first birthday you better never, ever pull a stunt like this again!"

As you turned and walked away, you had a flashback of your childhood and thought, "No! It can't be. I've turned into my father (or mother)." Contrary to your best intentions, you didn't do what *Andy* would do. You did what *Barney* would do.

101

This psychological phenomenon is called behavior modeling. Where did you learn to parent? From *your* parents. That modeling became part of your schema. In spite of your conscious decision to do otherwise, when the pressure was on you did what your parents did.

Since you didn't have another parent model (except Andy, which you knew wasn't reality) you *naturally reacted* to what was encoded in your schema when your teenager didn't make curfew. That's right, monkey see, monkey do. Stimulus, response. It's all part of your reward and punishment schema.

So how do you get this monkey off your back?

You can't beat your animal body into submission. It has a lifetime of conditioning and it craves its rewards and fears its punishments. Since your animal is well fed and conditioned, it's not going to submit easily. The key is not trying to beat your animal into submission. Religions have tried this. The result is failure, frustration, and a sense of helplessness and hopelessness.

You can't erase your reward and punishment schema but as you act on your purpose and experience its power, you create new neurological pathways. Intrinsic change is transformational because it is inside out instead of outside in. When you start acting on your purpose your superhuman becomes stronger.

These new neurological pathways develop your new purpose-based schema. Each time you repeat your new purpose-based behaviors you strengthen the connections between the neurons. The more repetitions, the stronger the connections. The more you repeat the behavior, the more ingrained the neurological pathways. You are creating new ruts.

When the new ruts become deeper than the old ones, your behavior changes. You make a schema-shift.

Your Eyes Can Deceive You

I've experienced the schema-shift I just described. It's an evolutionary process. That shift has resulted in me relying less on what I see with my *natural* eyes and relying more on what I see with my *supernatural* eyes. My radio receiver is tuned in more to the supernatural frequency of purpose as opposed to the natural signal of external stimuli. I make the effort. God delivers the results. The result is my superhuman is *leading* my animal instead of the other way around.

There's a scene in *Star Wars* where Luke Skywalker gets his first supernatural seeing lesson. He is learning to use his light saber under the tutelage of Obi-Wan (Ben) Kenobi while Han Solo looks on. Luke's sparring partner is a small, flying robotic remote that shoots stinging laser pulses at him while he attempts to deflect them with his light saber. The remote is scoring hits left and right and Luke gets frustrated. Ben encourages Luke to trust the supernatural power of the Force rather than relying on conscious effort:

Ben: Remember a Jedi can feel the Force flowing through him.

Luke: You mean it controls your actions?

Ben: Partially, but it also obeys your commands.

Han: Hokey religions and ancient weapons are no match for a good blaster at your side, kid.

Luke (to Han): You don't believe in the Force, do you?

Han: Kid, I've flown from one side of this galaxy to the other. I've seen a lot of strange stuff, but I've never seen anything to make me believe there's one all-powerful Force controlling everything. There's no mystical energy field that controls my destiny. It's all a lot of simple tricks and nonsense.

Ben: I suggest you try it again Luke. This time let go of your conscious self and act on instinct. Ben places a helmet on Luke's head with the blast-shield down to blind him, telling him: "Your eyes can deceive you. Don't trust them. Stretch out with your feelings." Luke calmly evades and

To prevent Luke from relying on his *natural* instincts Ben places a helmet on Luke's head with a blast-shield that serves as a blindfold, forcing him to rely on his *supernatural* instincts. Luke gives it another go with this advice from Ben: "Your eyes can deceive you. Don't trust them. Stretch out with your feelings." Now Luke easily outmaneuvers the flying robot, deflecting the light pulses with ease. It's his first lesson in relying on the power of the Force. "You've taken your first step into a larger world," Ben tells Luke.

Just like Luke, I'm learning to let the Force flow through me and guide my thoughts and actions. I'm learning to trust the power of the Force as it leads me into a larger world — a world that extends beyond what I experience with my five senses. My eyes may deceive me but I don't have to rely on my eyes. The Force guides me instead. That's how I would describe the shift from my old natural, reward and punishment schema to my new supernatural, purpose-based schema.

The more I trust the supernatural power of purpose the more I experience supernatural results. But that transformation is not immediate. It's a process. Luke's first brush with the power of the Force was just the beginning of an evolutionary process that moved him from a *natural* schema to a *supernatural* schema. Luke's transformation took time — two sequels to be exact. But operating in the supernatural eventually became natural for Luke.

In the early years of following the path of my purpose I had anxiety attacks. I had quit my job and given up all financial security. My first attempt at starting a business had failed. My darkest hours were when I didn't know what to do or how to do it. But that's when I started learning to trust the Force. How do you take a former cowboy and feed salesman with an animal science degree and transform him into a writer, professional speaker and management consultant? That's not natural — it's supernatural.

Let Your GPS Guide You

I flew into Dallas for a speaking engagement and rented a car. I asked the lady at the counter if she could give me directions to my hotel. She explained that my car was equipped with a Global Positioning System (GPS) that would direct me to my destination. She asked if I had ever used a GPS before. I pleaded ignorance so she said she would show me how.

As we walked to the car she said, "All you have to do is enter the address into the GPS and a voice will tell you exactly what to do." I told her this would be just like traveling with my wife. After she programmed my GPS I took off for the hotel. A voice — a female voice — started giving me directions. "She" told me where to turn, how far away my turn was and when I needed to change lanes and merge. A screen on the GPS showed my path as I drove.

The toughest thing for me to do was to trust the GPS. I listened to the voice but couldn't stop myself from looking at the map and the road signs. I'd go back and forth and on more than one occasion pulled off the road onto the shoulder. The voice patiently waited for me to decide what I wanted to do — trust my eyes or trust the voice. It was my choice.

When I pulled up in front of the hotel she told me I had arrived. It was amazing.

The transformation from the natural to supernatural is like learning to trust a GPS when you're conditioned to trust your own eyes. To follow the path of purpose you have to listen to your internal GPS. Think of it as your *God Positioning System*. Your superhuman is telling you to where to go.

When Luke is in a bind, he hears Ben's voice urging him, "Use the Force, Luke. Let go, Luke. Luke, trust me." That's what I started learning to do. I had to rely on God to guide me if I was going to fulfill my purpose. I learned he was on the inside of me looking out instead of outside looking in. I had to learn *not* to trust my eyes, to let go, to use the Force. I'm still in that evolutionary process but it gets easier as I continue to travel the path of purpose.

In movies like *Stars Wars* the supernatural is dramatized with high tech special effects. I've found the supernatural to be more, well, natural. In other words, it isn't Obi-Wan Kenobe's spirit appearing to me in a vision and giving me instructions. It's hearing God's instructions in my thoughts and realizing that *is* supernatural. The supernatural should be *normal* not paranormal.

I used to wonder how much of life is predestined and how much depends on our choices. I've come to believe it's both. Luke asks Ben if the Force controls him. "Partially," is his answer, "but it also obeys your commands."

Our relationship with God is a dynamic, interdependent relationship where only he sees the completeness of the big picture. That's why we have to understand God's purpose for us to truly understand God. I can only really trust God when I know what his purpose is for *me*. I can trust him because he wants me to succeed in my assignment.

I hate to contradict Stuart Smalley, but we'll never be good enough, smart enough and dog-gone it, some people just aren't going to like us. There is a good reason for our insecurity. We recognize that in and of ourselves we are incomplete. Our natural ability is limited. Our supernatural ability is unlimited. In *Quiet Moments with God,* Lloyd John Ogilvie points out that in the New Testament the word *perfect* means, "complete, mature, accomplishing our purpose." When we are on purpose, we are *perfect.* When we are on purpose everything we need to fulfill it, but lack in the natural, is summoned in the supernatural. The Force is with us.

It is only when I am fulfilling my purpose that I am complete. If I don't know God's purpose for me, then I'm like Luke in his sparring match with the flying remote — I'm trying, but my efforts are hit and miss. When I'm on purpose I am deadly with my light saber, because the Force is flowing through me.

The Stages of Change

The schema shift from natural to supernatural is a process. Since you are addicted to your old behavior pattern, you must develop a new one*. According to researchers, modification of addictive behaviors involves progression through these six stages*:

1.   Precontemplation
2.   Contemplation
3.   Preparation
4.   Action
5.   Maintenance
6.   Termination

Precontemplation is the stage at which there is no intention to change behavior in the foreseeable future. People in this stage are typically unaware or under-aware that they have a problem. If you aren't even aware that you have a purpose then you really have a problem. If you don't know what it is yet, then you still have a problem. Your desire or lack of desire to find your purpose is a good indicator of which of the six stages you are in.

It is natural for us to question the reason for our being. So, we are in one of two places if we don't know what our purpose is: 1) we are either consciously or subconsciously searching for it or 2) we have consciously or subconsciously given up and said this is as good as it gets. We won't search for something we don't believe exists.

In the *Contemplation stage*, we are aware that a problem exists and are seriously thinking about overcoming it but haven't made a commitment to take action. The problem in this stage is that we struggle to decide if we want to struggle. "Do I actually have a purpose? If so, how do I find it?" I've actually had people balk at seeking their purpose based on this reasoning, "What if I discover my purpose and it's something I don't *want* to do?" I actually received an email from someone who wrote, "I'm tempted to come to your workshop but I'm afraid if I found my purpose it would only mean more work." Would God create you for a purpose and

---

*Prochaska, James O., DiClemente, Carlo Cl, & Norcross, John C. (1992). In Serach of How Poeple Change: Applications to Addictive Behaviors. American Psychologist, 1102-1113

equip you with a $6 million physical plant just to make you miserable? Work, when it is in the fulfillment of your purpose, is enjoyable. Regardless of how much adversity you may encounter on the path of God's purpose for your life, you will find the journey to be far more exhilarating and gratifying than anything you can cook up.

Preparation is the stage in which people explore ways to take action to modify their behavior in the immediate future. We have people who come to our workshops who are professional explorers. They have made the rounds through every self-help seminar and program you can imagine. Some are self-confessed self-help junkies. They've read all the books and listened to all the tapes of all the motivational gurus. Others are religious junkies. They've read all the books and listened to all the tapes of every preacher and teacher. I've spent time in both camps. Even when I didn't know that I was searching for my purpose I knew I wasn't maximizing my potential. I kept looking for answers in the same places and I kept getting the same answers.

We are told that God has a purpose for us. But many of us find ourselves in the same place as Doug. Doug was a successful businessman but as he put it, "Money wasn't an issue any longer and things weren't an issue any longer and I was searching for something." Doug told me about his search for purpose, "I asked my mom, I asked my dad, I asked my uncles and I asked my preacher. Everybody had an answer but they didn't have an avenue for me to get the answer I needed." Doug was getting answers that described purpose in broad monolithic or general terms. Doug wanted to know what *his* purpose was but couldn't find anyone who could help him find it. Doug did find the answer he needed as one of our first institute participants.

Po Bronson discovered something I found to be interesting when he interviewed people for his book, *What Should I do With My Life?* Religion didn't necessarily offer an avenue, as Doug put it, for those looking for the answers they needed:

> *Half the people in this book are devout, and not once did that insulate them from struggling with the question of what to do with their life. Most of them sat down with their rector/pastor/father/guru and asked for guidance. Never did that bring them peace or settle their mind. Many spoke of how helpless their religious advisor seemed.*

Religion tends to *dictate* rather than *facilitate*. It's easier to give you answers rather than help you find them. Laws and rules are systemic. It's all yes/no, black/white, ought/should. But your purpose is not systemic. It can't be defined for you like a rule or a law. To borrow Doug's term, you need an avenue or a process to find your purpose. Your purpose is intrinsic. You already posses it, you just need to find it. And that takes us to the next stage.

The *Action* stage involves taking steps to modify our behavior, experiences, or environment to overcome problems. We may be searching for our purpose even if we wouldn't define it in those terms. It is the seeking — however we may define it — that sets everything in motion. Action is the catalyst for faith. Seek and you will find. Once you start seeking, what you are seeking starts seeking you. You may not know exactly what you are searching for but you have to start the search. I didn't know how to describe what I was seeking until I found it, or maybe to be more accurate, until it found me.

Knock and the door will be opened. I was inadvertently using the *corridor principle*. Imagine you are standing at the end of a long, narrow hallway. You can't see what doors are open until you start walking down the hallway. If you start walking, you'll find the open door. But you have to start walking. This book merely provides a process for the discovery. It starts you down the corridor, or avenue as Doug put it, to help you find the open door. In the words of Galileo, "You cannot teach a man anything; you can only help him find it for himself."

Maintenance is the stage where people work to prevent relapse and consolidate the gains made during the action stage. Now here's where the problem sets in according to the researchers. People often erroneously equate *action* with *change*. Oh, if it were only that easy. These stages do not progress in a straight line.The stages of change ascend and descend in a spiral effect. Precontemplation is followed by contemplation, then preparation and action. Then a relapse may occur. So it's back to contemplation, preparation and action again. This cycle may be repeated until maintenance of the desired change is achieved. This is the transformational power of purpose.

This process includes relapses — sometimes many relapses. For instance, how many smokers stop, start, stop, start, stop and start again before finally quitting all together? Action doesn't equal change. Maintenance of the new behavior equals change. That's when the new schema overtakes the old.

I was addicted to my old patterns of behavior dictated by my old natural, reward and punishment schema. I am building new neurological pathways as I act on my purpose and experience the results God delivers. I'm learning to trust the Force. The tug of war between my old and new schema continues but my new supernatural schema is more dominant. The connections between my neurons grow stronger as I experience the transformational power of purpose. The real you is set free as your supernatural schema overtakes your natural schema. The chains that kept you bound are broken and your superhuman is liberated.

Finding your purpose is the beginning of a new journey but it brings with it a sense of peace and reassurance. I like the way Doug said it, "If you can ever discover your purpose, you'll wake up in the morning feeling content, feeling happy, but not searching for the things you *can't* find."

Termination is the stage where there is no chance of relapse. For us, termination is when our animal body dies. It has served its function in this life. This is the ultimate liberation of our superhuman. We leave the natural habitat behind and now reside exclusively in the supernatural. Barbara Karnes describes this experience in her book, *Gone from My Sight*:

> *The separation becomes complete when breathing stops. What appears to be the last breath is often followed by one or two long spaced breaths and then the body is empty. The owner is no longer in need of a heavy nonfunctioning vehicle.*

> *How we approach death is going to depend upon our fear of life, and how willing we are to let go of this known expression to venture into a new one. Fear*

107

and unfinished business are two big factors in determining how much resistance we put into meeting death.

In *Tuesdays with Morrie*, Mitch is a successful sportswriter who discovers that Morrie, one of his old professors, is terminally ill. The film, based on Mitch Albom's bestselling book, revolves around the emotional bond formed by the two men leading up to Morrie's death. Morrie teaches Mitch about life while he is in the process of dying. Among the many bits of wisdom Morrie shares are a couple all of us should remember:

●. "Fear of aging... you know what that reflects, Mitch? Lives that haven't found meaning."

●. "If we accept the fact that we can die at any time we'd live our lives differently."

If we feel we have fulfilled our purpose in life we can accept death as the completion of our assignment on earth.

Take in a Movie

Throughout this book I've referred to scenes from several movies. The reason for this is that they are, for the most part, reference points from our popular culture that most of us can relate to. My intent is to evoke an emotion that correlates to a point I am making. This helps you *feel* rather than just *read* what I'm writing.

Literature and film allow us to vicariously experience life's powerful play through the lives of the characters. Their stories can provide us with timeless, heroic and meaningful examples of purpose.

I can remember watching *It's a Wonderful Life* when we were living in that rundown old farmhouse. I was moved to tears watching George Bailey struggling at the low point of his life — because I was struggling at the low point of my life. I could relate to George. I thought I had lost everything. I didn't know what to do. I wished I'd never been born. I saw my story in George Bailey's story and it gave me hope. *The Treasure of Sierra Madre* reminded me of my gold prospecting expedition. Again, I saw myself in the characters.

I want you to rent one or more of your favorite movies — not those mindless ones you rent just for laughs or pure entertainment — but those that really move you emotionally. It might be *Forrest Gump, Braveheart* or *Seabiscuit*. If you're like me, it might be one of the old classics.

As you watch, which of the characters do you relate to and why? What is it about the story that moves you? What are you experiencing or have experienced in your life that you can relate to on the screen?

Once again, record your responses below. And as always, write in as much detail as possible. Keep your book handy as you watch the movie. When you are particularly moved by a scene, pause the video, record your responses and then continue.

Take in a Movie: Continued

_____

_____

_____

_____

_____

_____

_____

_____

_____

_____

_____

_____

_____

_____

_____

_____

_____

_____

_____

_____

_____

Chapter 10

The Weakest Link

There's a scene from the movie *Patton* where the famous general has just been relieved of his command during World War II. Devastated by the news, he vents to his aide:

> *I feel I am destined to achieve some great thing. What, I don't know. But this last incident is so trivial in its nature and so terrible in its effect, it can't be the result of an accident. It has to be the work of God. The last great opportunity of a lifetime, an entire world at war and I'm not a part of it? God will not permit this to happen! I am going to be allowed to fulfill my destiny. His will be done!*

George Patton went on to play a pivotal role in the Battle of the Bulge, the battle that delivered the final, fatal blow to Nazi Germany. History holds a place for people on purpose. "The idea that this universe in all its million-fold order and precision is the result of blind chance is as credible as the idea that if a print shop blew up all the type would fall down again in the finished and faultless form of the dictionary," said Albert Einstein.

In *The Denial of Death*, Ernest Becker writes, "People are capable of the highest generosity and self-sacrifice. But they have to feel and believe what they are doing is truly heroic, timeless and supremely meaningful. The crisis of modern society is precisely that people no longer feel heroic."

You are here to do something timeless, truly heroic and meaningful. The transformational power of purpose sets you on a collision course with destiny.

What if You Had Never Been Born?

In the opening scenes of *It's a Wonderful Life*, God summons the angel Clarence to help George Bailey. Clarence asks if George is sick. "No," answers God. "It's worse, he's discouraged." George feels all is lost — his business, his family and his friends. He wonders aloud if it would have been better had he never been born. Clarence decides to show George what *would* have happened had he not been born. It has far-reaching effects in the lives of his family, his community and even the world.

George had saved his brother Harry's life after he had fallen through the ice when they were children. Harry grew up to become a fighter pilot in World War II and saved the lives of thousands of troops on a naval transport. But since George had never been born he wasn't there to save Harry and he drowned. "Every man on that transport died," explains Clarence. "Harry wasn't there to save them because you weren't there to save Harry."

Just like George Bailey you and I have a verse to contribute in life's powerful play. Your purpose has far-reaching effects that you may never realize in this lifetime. There is not enough reward and punishment in the world to keep you going in the face of defeat and discouragement. Purpose has been the thing that has kept me going when I have been discouraged. I know my purpose is my verse to deliver.

Your purpose is your verse to deliver. What if you'd never been born? What impact would it have in life's powerful play?

Everyone's verse is significant, as George Bailey discovered. He thought of his life as insignificant. It was only when he saw what would have happened had he not been born that he realized the far-reaching effects his verse had on life's powerful play.

Discourage can be defined as an "attempt to dissuade." *Courage*, on the other hand, is "mental or moral strength to venture, persevere, and withstand danger, fear or difficulty." Or, as John Wayne put it, "Courage is being afraid and saddling up anyway."

The single most destructive force in the fulfillment of our purpose is discouragement. It is the demon of discouragement that is sent to try and derail us on the path of God's purpose for our lives. No one is exempt from the potentially debilitating effects of discouragement. Comments found in Mother Teresa's writings reveal that at times even she seemed to feel abandoned by God:

- •. "I am told that God lives in me — and yet the reality of darkness and coldness and emptiness is so great that nothing touches my soul."
- •. "I want God with all the power of my soul — and yet between us there is a terrible separation."
- •. "I feel just that terrible pain of loss, of God not being God, of God not really existing."

Mother Teresa struggled with feelings of doubt, despair and discouragement. But when her purpose was revealed to her in 1946, she left the comfort of teaching in a convent school and went to the slums of Calcutta to care for the sick and the dying. She saddled up anyway.

Others who have played pivotal roles in the history of mankind have been plagued by feelings of despair. Abraham Lincoln struggled with bouts of depression so severe that at one point in his presidency he wrote, "If what I feel were equally distributed to the whole human family there would not be one cheerful face on earth. Whether or not I shall be better I cannot tell. I awfully forbode that I shall not live. I have done nothing to make a single human being remember that I have lived."

But Lincoln also believed in the power of destiny, "There is a divinity that shapes our ends." It's hard to imagine how history might have been altered if Lincoln had been slain prematurely by the dagger of discouragement. He not only served as president during the most difficult chapter of our nation's history, he issued the Emancipation Proclamation, which ended slavery in the United States.

It was Henry David Thoreau's famous essay, *Civil Disobedience,* which influenced Martin Luther King, Jr. in his fight against desegregation. King would lead peaceful demonstrations to help win civil rights for the descendants of the slaves Lincoln freed a century earlier. It would take a hundred years for Lincoln's legacy to be fully realized, aided by the influence of Thoreau. Thoreau died in 1862 and Lincoln was assassinated in 1865. Both contributed critical and timely verses to life's powerful play. Neither lived to see the full impact their lives had on history.

When we look at the lives of Lincoln, Thoreau and Mother Teresa, we have to wonder, "What if?" What if they hadn't contributed their verses to life's powerful play?

We can't see everything destiny has in store for us. Remember the corridor principle. It is only as we walk down the corridor that we see the open doors. There are several good reasons why the path of God's purpose for your life is revealed incrementally. One is that you and I can only handle so much without shouting, "Overload! This is too much information. I don't see how I can possibly do everything I'm supposed to do!" Another reason would be our knowing in advance what difficulties lay in our paths and to *not* try to avoid them. "It is a mistake to look too far ahead," said Winston Churchill. "Only one link of the chain of destiny can be handled at a time."

I had no idea what I was getting into when I discovered my purpose. It has only been in retrospect that I have been able to put the pieces of the purpose puzzle together. During that time, I have experienced a lot of adversity. Life has not been easy. But life wasn't easy before I discovered my purpose either.

Anything worthwhile is *never* easy. And when I get discouraged and think that I'd like to live a "normal" life again, I ask myself, "Why would I want to do that?" I like the challenge of purposeful living. It's an adventure. Like the Blues Brothers, I'm on a mission for God.

The path of purpose is not static, it's dynamic. It's up and down.

There's a great scene from the movie *Parenthood* that puts the ups and downs into perspective. The film revolves around the lives of several generations of a family experiencing the good, the bad and the ugly of dealing with kids, siblings, parents and grandparents. Steve Martin, who plays the role of a father who is about at the end of his rope, is venting to his wife about how messy their lives are. And like many of us, he doesn't like messy. His grandmother overhears the conversation and offers this jewel of wisdom:

> *You know, when I was nineteen grandpa took me on a rollercoaster. Up, down, up, down. Oh, what a ride! I always wanted to go again. You know it was interesting to me that a ride could make me so frightened, so scared, so sick, so excited and so thrilled altogether. Some didn't like it. They went on the merry-go-round. That just goes around. Nothing. I like the rollercoaster. You get more out of it.*

The road *most* traveled is a merry-go-round. Nothing. It just goes around. Quiet desperation. The path of purpose is the road *less* traveled, a rollercoaster. I'm with grandma. I like the rollercoaster better. You get more out of it.

It's a Small World

Your life affects the lives of many people — even those with whom you may never meet or come in contact with. As Clarence told George Bailey, "Strange isn't it? Each man's life touches so many other lives. When he isn't around he leaves an awful hole doesn't he?"

Psychologist Stanley Milgram conducted an experiment in the 1960s designed to see if randomly selected people would be able to find a specific person they did not know using only a network of friends. Two studies were conducted. One originated in Wichita, Kansas and the other in Omaha, Nebraska. Groups of people in each of these cities would try to connect with specifically identified people in Cambridge, Massachusetts. The people in Wichita and Omaha were each given a document folder that contained the following:

- •. The name, address and some personal data on the target person in Cambridge.
- •. A set of rules that included this specific directive: "If you do not know the target person on a first name basis, then pass the document folder on to one friend that you feel is most likely to know the target. That friend must be someone you know on a first-name basis."
- •. A roster for each person who got the folder to put their name on the list. This showed who it came from and kept the folder from making any loops.
- •. Tracer cards for each person who transmitted the folder to fill out and mail in.

It took a median of five intermediate friends to go from the starter to the target person. The results led Milgram to conclude that any two people in the world can be connected through a chain of no more than six other people. You've probably heard of it referred to as "six degrees of separation." The entire population of the United States could be connected through a series of a half-dozen handshakes with the person on one end of the chain of six not being personally acquainted with the person on the other end. It really is a small world after all and you are a critical link in the chain that connects us all.

Imagine the supernatural power of purpose multiplied through these six degrees of separation. It would have the effect of chain lightening. Your purpose affects the lives of not just one but possibly millions.

The Tsunami Effect

Acting on your purpose can be likened to an earthquake in the middle of the ocean. Powerful tidal waves of concentric circles expand from the epicenter created by the inertia of the quake driving them long distances with great force. When you act on your purpose it can have effects of seismic proportions.

I've had occasions to see the tsunami effect of acting on my purpose. This used to surprise me but not anymore. I ask God to direct me as I act on my purpose. He always delivers the results. It might be someone who writes me after a speaking engagement and tells me what I said that day was especially for them. And it's not just when I'm writing, speaking or consulting that I'm fulfilling my purpose of helping people reach their full potential. On my way to and from speaking engagements, I'll end up sitting on the plane next to someone by divine appointment. As we strike up a conversation it becomes evident I'm there to "help them reach their full potential."

I never know how God will deliver the results. Remember Mike, the young salesman who provided the inspiration for the discovery of my purpose? Mike not only went on to become a successful salesman, today he is the owner of his own company. Twelve years after I left Purina I was delivering a speech to the American Feed Industry Association and I shared the story about how Mike served as the catalyst for the discovery of my purpose.

Afterwards, one of the audience members came up to visit with me. He was one of the young salesmen I had worked with at Purina years ago and was now the vice-president of another company. He shared something with me that validates the power of the tsunami effect I just described, "Jim, do you know I have a copy of the ten questions Jim Whitt said to ask a feedlot manager on the first call? We made copies for all of the salesmen we worked with." He also told me that he gives all of the salespeople in his company a copy of my ten questions.

I had been fulfilling my purpose of helping people reach their full potential in ways I hadn't even known, and found out about it twelve years after the fact. That's the *tsunami effect* of purpose.

I received a letter from Shane who found a copy of *Road Signs For Success*, the first book I'd written, in a box of junk:

I'm writing this letter to you to tell you how much I have enjoyed Road Signs For Success. Your book has changed my life in the way I perceive problems and people around me. I recently went into business for myself. I have pushed for this goal for the last seven years. Truth be known, I waited so long because of fear.

Life had presented the situation of "Do or Die" and I went for it. Things are going great! I already have more work than I can handle. My wife is able to stay home with the children and we are happier about life. I received your book from a man my wife worked with 3 to 4 years ago. He told us, "Here take this stuff or I'm throwing it out." We took the stuff and your book was in it.

At first I was skeptical... motivational mumbo-jumbo and ridiculed it. Then I read a little, and then a little more. Finally I could not put it down. Since that time I have read the book at least 3 times and refer to it often. My wife calls it

115

my bible. And in many ways it does remind me of my grandmother's Bible. The spine is broken, the cover is worn and pages sometimes fall out.

I called the phone number on Shane's letterhead and his wife answered. Shane was out of the office but his wife shared the rest of his story with me. She explained that her husband had been diagnosed as bipolar and had been completely unmotivated until my book found its way into his hands. Learning that my book was relegated to a box of junk didn't exactly make my day, but Shane's letter is proof positive that one man's trash is another man's treasure. He needed that book and God put it in his hands, albeit in an unconventional manner. It inspired him to overcome his fear and take the leap of faith.

As Dolly Parton said, "Sometimes it's funny the way we find inspiration."

I've stopped trying to figure out where the path of purpose leads. I always wanted to experience "real" faith. Well, be careful of what you wish for because you might get it. That wish landed me in a rundown old farmhouse. But it was there I learned real faith. It's best described by St. Augustine, "Faith is to believe what we do not see; and the reward of this faith is to see what we believe." I don't have to know the outcome. That's not my job. My job is to act on my purpose. It's God's job to deliver the results.

Living like this can be scary. When we were living in that old farmhouse, I didn't have any idea how I was going to make it. I didn't have any idea how I was going to care for my family. But I saddled up anyway. And as I walk the path of God's purpose for my life, I've discovered that what I need will be waiting for me when I need it. It's comfortable yet uncomfortable.

How can you be comfortable and uncomfortable at the same time? I like the way Olympian Michael Johnson explains it. He was asked if he was nervous in the starting blocks after he had just beaten his own world record, "I was nervous and when I'm nervous I'm comfortable." He knows that being nervous is normal if you are preparing to run a big race. And being on purpose is running a big race.

Your Date With Destiny

As a teenager, I spent some of my summers working for wheat farmers. After the wheat was harvested, the next item on the agenda was plowing the ground to prepare the soil for next year's crop. Most fields were plowed from the outside in — making the first round on the outer edge of the field and circling inward with each succeeding round. In Oklahoma, it's a hot summer wind that comes sweeping down the plains and saps the soil of its moisture. To get the ground plowed before it became too dry and hard, we often plowed around the clock.

I much preferred plowing during the day even though it meant riding the tractor in the scorching afternoon sun. The unplowed ground disappeared before your eyes. I always felt a great sense of accomplishment watching the field turn from the golden brown color of the wheat stubble to the rich blackness of the newly plowed earth. It's easy to stay with a task when you can see you're making progress.

But plowing at night was different. The only part of the field that was visible was the area illuminated by the tractor's headlights and one light mounted on a rear fender trained on the plow behind the tractor. The rest of the field was enveloped in darkness. When plowing the night shift I would start before sunset and would finish my shift twelve hours later just after the sun came up. The thing I always hated about plowing at night was not being able to see the field shrink with each round. In the large fields it seemed as though I was stuck in the same spot. The hours passed slowly and in the middle of the night I fought boredom and sleep. Those were the longest nights I can ever remember in my life. I have to admit there were times I was tempted to park the tractor and take a nap. But I kept the plow in the ground and the throttle wide open.

Finally the pitch black of night turned to the gray light of dawn. As the sun peaked over the horizon it threw a stream of light across the field catching the tops of the furrows. The fruits of several hours of labor were no longer cloaked in the secrecy of darkness but were revealed in the early light of day. It was only then that I felt that sense of accomplishment, because it was only then that I could see the results. I was making progress all through the night but simply couldn't see the results.

None of us knows when our journey in this world will come to an end. Our days are numbered — we just don't know what that number is. The average life span in America is about 75 years of age now. Take 75 times 365 and you've got 27,375 days to live. If you are on the low side of that figure here's what I want you to do. Take your age in years and multiply it times 365. That will give you the days that you have behind you. Now subtract that number from 75. How many days do you have left?

That's a sobering thought isn't it?

There's an old Chinese proverb that says a journey of a thousand leagues begins with a single step. When you started reading this book you made a decision to start the process of finding your purpose and fulfilling it. That was the first step. After you discover your purpose you are then confronted with another question. Will you say yes to your purpose? "Destiny is not a matter of chance," said William Jennings Bryan, "it is a matter of choice." It's one thing to be presented with our date with destiny, it's another to say yes to it. You will be presented with that choice every day for as long as you live. What will you say when presented with that choice?

Traveling the path of God's purpose for your life can be likened to plowing a field. God has given you a purpose in life — a field to plow. When you know your purpose, you know you're plowing in the right field.

I discovered my purpose in life when I was 35 years, 6 months and 16 days old. That would be day number 12,198 of my 27,375 days. I did a lot of plowing up until that time, but I'm not sure all of it was in the right field. I *know* I've been plowing in the right field since then.

"Perseverance is not a long race. It is many short races one after another," says Walter Elliott in his book *Many Mistakes*. Plowing is a lot like that. You make many rounds with the tractor. Each round is like a short race. After you've completed many rounds or short races the big race is complete and the field is finished. You plow a field one round at a time. You fulfill your purpose one day at time. At times, you'll feel like you're plowing at night. But you can persevere when you're on purpose. The results are there — sometimes you just can't see them.

Destiny is counting on *you*. Don't park your tractor. Put your plow in the ground and throw the throttle wide open.

Your Purpose

Your responses to the exercises in this book and the supernatural insights you have received have provided the clues that will lead you to the discovery of your purpose. Think of them as pieces of the puzzle of the picture of your purpose. Now that you have all the pieces the only thing left for you to do is to put them together. This exercise is designed to help you do that.

This is the heavy-lifting exercise in the process of discovering your purpose. It will take some time so don't become overly anxious or discouraged if the pieces of your purpose puzzle don't fall into place immediately.

Go back through your responses to all of the exercises you've completed in this book. Underline or highlight any recurring phrases or themes you find. You will probably notice there is a common thread of words, phrases or thoughts that crop up throughout your exercises.

Summarize your conclusions here. Don't try to narrow your conclusions too much. Write out the recurring themes and phrases again. Remember when we started we compared the process to the game of Clue. You are looking for all the clues you can find that will lead you to your purpose.

_____

_____

_____

_____

_____

_____

_____

_____

_____

_____

_____

_____

_____

Your Purpose: Continued

Go back and circle any reoccurring words that you find. Record those words below. Now play the word game. For example, if you found that you used the word "freedom" repeatedly, write out what freedom means to you. Go to the dictionary and look at the definitions of freedom. Write them down. Do this with any words that you find repeatedly in your exercises or any words that just "jump out" at you as you reread them.

_____

_____

_____

_____

_____

_____

_____

_____

Now, as you consider what you've just written, what do you think your purpose might be? Write it in the space below. Think destination instead of vehicles. Remember that purpose is the "why" not the "how" or "what." Remember the four critical elements of purpose — it should be Positive, Powerful, Simple and Serving. Don't worry about whether or not you write the "right" answer. Relax, and let the Force take over. Just express your purpose to the best of your ability at this point.

_____

_____

_____

_____

_____

_____

What Now?

I believe the power of writing my purpose down on a sheet of paper was the equivalent of signing the contract for its fulfillment. God has delivered everything I have needed in the fulfillment of that contact. So please, write your purpose down. Again, don't worry about whether or not what you write is "right." Write it down and ruminate, meditate and regurgitate. If what you write isn't exactly right it will eventually lead you to what is right. I encourage you to rewrite your purpose using different verbiage until the light bulb comes on and you say, "That's it!" Just remember PPSS.

If, after reading this book and completing the exercises you're still unsure that you know exactly what your purpose is, take heart. We've had people call, e-mail or write us weeks and even months after attending a workshop to inform us that they found it. When you started this process you set supernatural principles into motion. Seek and you'll find. Keep seeking. You've got an assignment to fulfill on planet earth. God did not create you for a purpose to keep it hidden from you. Remember, it's OK to struggle. There's value in the struggle.

You'll receive more supernatural insights as you travel the path of purpose. You'll receive inspired ideas. Do not take them lightly. Write them down. God is giving you the guidance you asked for when you started the process.

Remember that *action* is the catalyst for faith. Act on your purpose and people and circumstances will come to you so that you may fulfill your purpose.

Be prepared for adversity. The path of purpose is not easy but it hurts so good! Take heart in the knowledge that adversity is the fire that refines the potential God entrusted to you.

There is indeed a superhuman in you. We are a superhuman race, extensions of God himself. You were put here on earth at a specific time to fulfill a specific purpose. Supernatural forces will come to your aid when you say yes to your date with destiny.

The supernatural will become more natural. As Obi-Wan told Luke. "You've taken your first step into a larger world." May the Force be with you!

•••

PS: I want to hear from you when you find your purpose. Email me about your experience at jim@whittenterprises.com.

Jim's responses to the exercise on page 47:

Martin Luther King, Jr. – To free the oppressed.
Mother Teresa – To love the unlovable.
Albert Einstein – To reveal the mind of God.
Bill Gates – To help people maximize their potential.
Oprah – To help people overcome obstacles in their lives.

About Jim Whitt

A native Oklahoman, Jim Whitt grew up working on ranches, farms and feedlots. After graduating from Oklahoma State University with a degree in animal science, he became a top producing salesman and marketing executive with two Fortune 500 companies. Jim's purpose-based philosophy was birthed when he discovered his purpose in life: "To help people reach their full potential." That discovery led to the founding of Whitt Enterprises LLC, a firm that helps people and organizations reach their full potential and The Institute for Purposeful Living, a nonprofit organization that helps people find and fulfill their purpose in life.

You can learn more about Jim's speaking and consulting at:

www.JimWhitt.com
PO Box 700897 • Tulsa, OK • 74170
918-494-0009 • Fax 918-494-0933

Other Books by Jim Whitt

Riding for the Brand:
The Power of Purposeful Leadership

Road Signs for Success:
99 Powerful Principles to Guide You
On The Road to Reaching Your Full Potential

CPSIA information can be obtained
at www.ICGtesting.com
Printed in the USA
BVHW052211120620
581226BV00008B/282